The American Dream in John Steinbeck's *Of Mice and Men*

Other Books in the Social Issues in Literature Series:

Social Issues
in Literature

The American Dream in John Steinbeck's *Of Mice and Men*

Hayley Mitchell Haugen, Book Editor

GREENHAVEN PRESS
A part of Gale, Cengage Learning

GALE
CENGAGE Learning

Detroit • New York • San Francisco • New Haven, Conn • Waterville, Maine • London

Christine Nasso, *Publisher*
Elizabeth Des Chenes, *Managing Editor*

© 2010 Greenhaven Press, a part of Gale, Cengage Learning

Gale and Greenhaven Press are registered trademarks used herein under license.

For more information, contact:
Greenhaven Press
27500 Drake Rd.
Farmington Hills, MI 48331-3535
Or you can visit our Internet site at gale.cengage.com

For product information and technology assistance, contact us at

Gale Customer Support, 1-800-877-4253
For permission to use material from this text or product, submit all requests online at
www.cengage.com/permissions

Further permissions questions can be emailed to permissionrequest@cengage.com

Articles in Greenhaven Press anthologies are often edited for length to meet page requirements. In addition, original titles of these works are changed to clearly present the main thesis and to explicitly indicate the author's opinion. Every effort is made to ensure that Greenhaven Press accurately reflects the original intent of the authors. Every effort has been made to trace the owners of copyrighted material.

Cover image copyright © Hulton Deutsh Collection/Corbis.

LIBRARY OF CONGRESS CATALOGING-IN-PUBLICATION DATA

The American dream in John Steinbeck's of Mice and men / Hayley Mitchell Haugen, book editor.
    p. cm. -- (Social issues in literature)
    Includes bibliographical references and index.
    ISBN 978-0-7377-4848-2 (hardcover) -- ISBN 978-0-7377-4849-9 (pbk.)
    1. Steinbeck, John, 1902-1968. Of mice and men. 2. National characteristics, American, in literature. 3. Social values in literature. I. Haugen, Hayley Mitchell, 1968-
    PS3537.T3234O39 2010
    813'.52--dc22
                                                                    2010004589

Printed in the United States of America
1 2 3 4 5 6 7 14 13 12 11 10

Contents

Chapter 1: Background on John Steinbeck

Chapter 2: *Of Mice and Men* and the American Dream

Many of Steinbeck's works strive to interpret the American scene. In particular, *Of Mice and Men* portrays characters searching for the promise of America, only to be frustrated in their efforts. Ultimately, they strive for freedom and dignity in the face of constant change.

Chapter 3: Contemporary Perspectives on the American Dream

Introduction

When John Steinbeck was awarded the Nobel Prize for Literature in 1962, in his brief acceptance speech he admitted, "In my heart there may be doubt that I deserve the Nobel Award over other men of letters whom I hold in respect or reverence." While he may have doubted his worthiness for the award, it is clear that Steinbeck had no doubts about his role as a writer. The writer, he declared in his speech, is "charged with exposing our many grievous faults and failures, with dredging up to the light our dark and dangerous dreams for the purpose of improvement.... The writer is delegated to declare and to celebrate man's proven capacity for greatness of heart and spirit—for gallantry in defeat, for courage, compassion and love."

Steinbeck fulfills this charge time and time again in his works that expose both the joys and the hardships of ordinary people. Published in 1937, Steinbeck's novel *Of Mice and Men*, for instance, depicts the lives of two migrant farmworkers: George and his mentally disabled companion Lennie. Lonely travelers but loyal friends, the two men struggle to achieve their American dream of home and land ownership in California's Salinas Valley. Though determined to reach their goals, harsh living conditions, meager wages, and Lennie's disability ultimately prevent the men from gaining the kind of American independence and self-sufficiency they seek.

Upon the publication of *Of Mice and Men*, America was in the midst of the Great Depression, an economic crisis that left 25 percent of Americans jobless. At this time, the American reading public was certainly sympathetic and receptive to the novel's theme of thwarted dreams. Readers were so receptive, in fact, that the novel became an immediate best seller, selling 117,000 copies prior to its release date. According to the Martha Heasley Cox Center for Steinbeck Studies, *Of Mice and*

Men was also an immediate selection for the Book of the Month Club, and it has since been translated into multiple languages. Upon its release, Hollywood producers also clamored for the chance to produce the work for both stage and screen. Steinbeck revised the novel slightly for the stage, and the work was ready for the theater by November 1937. Innumerable productions of the play have been staged since that time. As of 2010, three film versions of *Of Mice and Men* have also been made. The first movie adaptation screened in 1939, and the others appeared in 1981 (as a made-for-television movie) and in 1992.

In addition to being successful in print, stage, and film, *Of Mice and Men* is notable for its notoriety. According to the American Library Association, some of Steinbeck's initial readers were offended by the unrefined characters' occasional use of vulgar language and racial slurs. Throughout the years, other readers have condemned the book for George's unapologetic killing of Lennie, and even for the novel's stance against big business. The novel has, at times, been banned from American public and school libraries, and it has fallen within the sights of censors so frequently that it has made the American Library Association's list of the Most Frequently Challenged Books.

It is not for its cultural success and controversy alone, however, that *Of Mice and Men* has remained a popular fixture in the American literary canon, especially in America's high schools. According to the Martha Heasley Cox Center for Steinbeck Studies, *Of Mice and Men* "has the unique ability to capture an important period in American history while containing values that transcend specific time frames and cultures. Moreover, the characters in *Of Mice and Men* show a difficult truth about loneliness and an unreachable dream— something that most people, no matter their nationality or social station, can identify with." The novel's transcendence of time is especially relevant when considering the economic crisis that began in 2008, the worst recession since the Great Depression. With nearly 10 percent of Americans out of work in 2009, American citizens were losing their homes at a record rate. According to Reuters news service, the foreclosure activity for June 2009 was the third highest on record, and the fourth straight month of filings on more than three hundred thousand properties. Americans began to wonder what happened to their American dream.

John Steinbeck's *Of Mice and Men* reminds today's readers that they are not alone in their struggles to attain or regain their American dream. Indeed, through his creation of George and Lennie, Steinbeck illustrates that he understood America's plight. In her short online essay "Why Read John Steinbeck?" Susan Shillinglaw, a professor of English at San Jose State University and scholar-in-residence at the National Steinbeck Center in Salinas, suggests that this understanding stems from Steinbeck's being attuned to the internal landscape of man. This landscape, Shillinglaw says, is often "shaped by isolation, loneliness, [and] failure," but "his is never the language of despair but of empathy." Steinbeck endures, Shillinglaw says, because he "embraces the fullness of life. With compassion, tolerance, and humility, he surveys landscapes: of place, of spirit, of a nation."

The articles that follow provide insight into Steinbeck's compassion, tolerance, and humility through their exploration of the American dream in *Of Mice and Men*. Chapter 1 places the novel in biographical and historical context. Chapter 2 offers literary criticism on characters, setting, themes, motifs, and other elements of fiction within the novel, relating specifically to the theme of the American dream. Finally, Chapter 3 of this volume contains current viewpoints on the American dream and its significance in contemporary American culture.

Chronology

1902

John Ernst Steinbeck Jr. is born to Olive and John Steinbeck in Salinas, California, on February 27.

1919

Steinbeck graduates from Salinas High School.

1920

Steinbeck enrolls as an English major at Stanford University in California.

1925

Steinbeck leaves Stanford without completing a degree and works for the *New York American*, a New York City newspaper, for a year before returning to California.

1929

Cup of Gold is published by Robert M. McBride.

1930

Steinbeck marries Carol Henning and moves to Pacific Grove, California.

1932

The Pastures of Heaven is published by Brewer, Warren, and Putnam.

1933

To a God Unknown is published by Robert O. Ballou.

1934

Steinbeck's mother dies.

1935

Steinbeck's father dies; *Tortilla Flat* is published by Covici-Friede and wins a gold medal from the Commonwealth Club of California.

1936

In Dubious Battle is published by Covici-Friede.

1937

Of Mice and Men is published by Covici-Friede as both a novella and a play (the play wins the New York Drama Critics' Circle Award); *The Red Pony* is published by Covici-Friede; Steinbeck takes his first trip to Europe.

1938

The publishing house of Covici-Friede goes bankrupt, and Covici joins the publishers at Viking. *The Long Valley* and *Their Blood Is Strong* are published by Viking.

1939

The Grapes of Wrath is published by Viking; Steinbeck is elected to the National Institute of Arts and Letters.

1940

Steinbeck wins the Pulitzer Prize for *The Grapes of Wrath*. Film versions are made of *The Grapes of Wrath* and *Of Mice and Men*.

1941

The Sea of Cortez is published by Viking.

1942

Bombs Away and *The Moon Is Down* are published by Viking.

1943

Steinbeck and Carol Henning divorce, and he marries Gwyndolen Conger. He goes to Europe as a war correspondent for the *New York Herald Tribune*.

1944
Steinbeck's first son, Thom, is born August 2.

1945
Cannery Row is published by Viking.

1946
Steinbeck's second son, John IV, is born June 12.

1947
The Pearl and *The Wayward Bus* are published by Viking.

1948
Steinbeck and Gwyndolen Conger divorce; Steinbeck is elected to the American Academy of Arts and Letters.

1949
The Red Pony is made into a film.

1950
Burning Bright is published as both a novel and a play by Viking; Steinbeck marries Elaine Scott.

1952
East of Eden is published by Viking; Steinbeck reports as a war correspondent from Europe for *Collier's* magazine.

1954
Sweet Thursday is published by Viking.

1957
The Short Reign of Pippin IV is published by Viking.

1958
Once There Was a War, a collection of wartime dispatches, is published by Viking.

1960

Steinbeck takes a three-month tour of the United States with his poodle, Charley.

1961

The Winter of Our Discontent is published by Viking. Steinbeck suffers a minor heart attack or stroke.

1962

Travels with Charley: In Search of America is published by Viking; Steinbeck wins the Nobel Prize for Literature.

1963

Steinbeck tours Europe with American playwright Edward Albee under the Department of State's Cultural Exchange program.

1964

Steinbeck is presented the United States Medal of Freedom by President Lyndon B. Johnson.

1966

America and Americans is published by Viking. The John Steinbeck Society of America is founded.

1968

Steinbeck dies in New York City on December 20.

CHAPTER 1

Background on
John Steinbeck

John Steinbeck:
The Man and His Work

Contemporary Literary Criticism Select

John Steinbeck is one of America's most significant writers of the twentieth century. As noted in the following selection, Steinbeck is remembered for both his forceful writing style and his compassion for the disadvantaged. The authors argue that Steinbeck's novels most often portray characters in relationship to their environments. In Steinbeck's Of Mice and Men, *a novel that rapidly achieved success, two itinerant farmhands seek out a living on the farms of California's Salinas Valley, a frequent setting for Steinbeck's works. George and his mentally disabled sidekick, Lennie, come close to achieving their American dream of purchasing a farm, but this dream is shattered when Lennie accidentally kills their boss's son's wife. This plot has encouraged multiple critical interpretations, the authors explain. Some critics read the novel allegorically as a retelling of the biblical Cain and Abel story. Others read it as a social critique that reflects Steinbeck's philosophical views.*

Best known for his controversial Pulitzer Prize–winning novel, *The Grapes of Wrath* (1939), John Steinbeck is considered among the most significant American novelists of the twentieth century. When he was honored in 1962 with the Nobel Prize in literature, the awards committee cited Steinbeck's "sympathetic humor and sociological perception" and his "instinct for what is genuinely American, be it good or bad." In his fiction, Steinbeck professed both sympathy and anger toward American society. An active opponent of social exploitation, puritanism, and materialistic values, Steinbeck is noted for his sharp, forceful writing style, his wry humor, and his profound compassion for the poor, the inarticulate, and the politically maligned.

Early in his career, as a result of his study of biology at Stanford University during the 1920s, Steinbeck developed a "biological" view of humanity. He insisted that such evolutionary concepts as adaptation and natural selection apply to human society and that more profound observations could be gleaned from examining people in groups than as individuals. Steinbeck's characters usually live in harmony with nature until such malevolent political or natural forces as progress, scarcity, or drought upset that balance. Through mutual cooperation, the will to adapt, and a mystical religious faith in the power of the just individual, Steinbeck's characters are usually able to survive destructive circumstances.

Many of Steinbeck's novels and stories are set in and around the Salinas Valley in California, where he was born and where he held a variety of jobs prior to his writing career. He often used this setting to stress his theme of the importance of the "relationship between man and his environment," [critic] Peter Shaw claimed. "The features of the valley at once determined the physical fate of his characters and made symbolic comment on them." Moreover, while Steinbeck dwelled on the beauty and "fruitfulness" of the valley, he "did not make it a fanciful Eden," Shaw commented. "The river brought destructive floods as well as fertility, and the summer wind could blow hot for months without let-up." Thus, "Man struggled within a closed system that both formed and limited him; there he was responsible for his acts and yet unable to control the larger forces." . . .

Of Mice and Men

Steinbeck gained national recognition with *Of Mice and Men* (1937), a pastoral novel which addresses such themes as the conflict between idealism and reality and the loneliness which divides people of all classes. This work centers on two itinerant ranch hands—Lennie, a strong retarded man, and George, who looks after Lennie and dreams of owning a small farm. After Lennie accidentally kills the conniving wife of his employer's son, George mercifully kills Lennie to spare him a crueler death by a lynch mob. Steinbeck adapted the novel for the Broadway stage in 1937 to great popular and critical acclaim. The drama, for which Steinbeck received a New York Drama Critics Circle Award, was described by Stark Young as an "absorbing work of theater art," by Brooks Atkinson as "a masterpiece," and by John Mason Brown as "one of the finest, most pungent, and most poignant realistic productions." . . .

Steinbeck began writing *Of Mice and Men* in January 1936. Like his previous novel *In Dubious Battle*, the characters and setting for *Of Mice and Men* are derived from his experiences as a farm laborer in California in 1922. Originally entitled "Something That Happened," *Of Mice and Men* was completed during the summer and published in February 1937. Although Steinbeck did not expect the novel to do well, *Of Mice and Men* appeared on best-seller lists from April into the fall, allowing him to finance his first trip to Europe. Upon returning to the United States in August, he worked with George Kaufman on the theater adaptation of the novel, which required few changes. With Kaufman as director, the play opened in New York at the Music Box Theatre in November 1937 and won the Drama Critics Circle Award over plays that included Thornton Wilder's *Our Town*.

Of Mice and Men relates the experiences of itinerant field hands Lennie Small and George Milton over a three-day period. Simpleminded and gentle, Lennie possesses great physical strength and becomes unwittingly destructive when startled. He relies upon George for guidance as the pair move from one ranch to another. Rather than squander their earnings in town saloons and whorehouses, the two workers try to save money in the hope of eventually buying property of their

Nobel Prize winner John Steinbeck (second from the left) investigates the conflict of reality and idealism in his novel Of Mice and Men. *AP Images.*

own. They find work on a ranch and meet a coworker who offers his savings to help finance the purchase of a farm. Before the acquisition can be made, however, Lennie unintentionally kills the coquettish wife of the boss's son when her frightened reaction to his innocent overtures scares him. George finds Lennie in hiding and shoots him—knowing that the lynch mob would have murdered Lennie in a more cruel and frightening fashion. The novel concludes as George walks to town to spend his money, abandoning his dream of buying a farm. For the stage version, Steinbeck expanded the role of the flirtatious wife and altered the conclusion so that the play ends just before Lennie's death.

Critical Response to *Of Mice and Men*

Of Mice and Men has engendered surprisingly diverse interpretations, considering its length and ostensible simplicity.

Much of the criticism perceives the story to be either an allegory or a tragedy. Critics who consider the story allegorical point to the contrasts between George and Lennie as the key to interpreting the novel. For example, some consider George representative of the rationality of the mind and Lennie representative of the appetites of the body; accordingly they interpret Lennie's dependence on George and the necessity for George to kill Lennie as the mind's responsibility for the actions of the body. Other critics who consider the novel allegorical argue that Steinbeck based *Of Mice and Men* on the biblical tale of Cain and Abel, in which Cain is banished from his family to wander alone, and interpret George's loss of Lennie as Steinbeck's confirmation of the individual's destiny to live in isolation. Commentators who view *Of Mice and Men* as a tragedy emphasize the seemingly fated end of the sole friendship in the novel and George's abandonment of a noble dream despite the standing offer of assistance from a coworker. A few observers, however, have responded that George and Lennie lack tragic character flaws and that Steinbeck's use of foreshadowing de-emphasizes the characters' ability to make choices, therefore mitigating any sense of tragedy in the classic tradition.

Other areas of critical concern include discussion of the novel as social criticism, realism, and as a reflection of Steinbeck's philosophical views. Although most critics agree that Steinbeck did not intend *Of Mice and Men* to be social criticism on the same level as *In Dubious Battle* or *The Grapes of Wrath*, the novel nonetheless describes the aimless existence of migrant laborers who work hard yet perpetually lack the money to purchase farms of their own. Many observers have noted the realism of the work as well, particularly Steinbeck's rendering of the farm workers' speech and prosaic lives. However, a few ardent detractors have insisted that *Of Mice and Men* is an overtly theatrical, sentimental melodrama which does little more than arouse a reader's sympathy. *Of Mice and*

Men has also been perceived as the embodiment of a non-teleological philosophy, according to which events are beyond humankind's comprehension and control: despite the efforts of George and Lennie, their plans fail and two people senselessly die. Noting that the original title of the novel was simply "Something That Happened," Peter Lisca has argued that "the ending of the story is . . . neither tragic nor brutal but simply a part of the pattern of events."

Steinbeck's Experience as a Ranch Hand Informed *Of Mice and Men*

Jay Parini

Jay Parini is D.E. Axinn Professor of English and Creative Writing at Middlebury College in Vermont. His book John Steinbeck: A Biography *was published in 1994, and his reviews and essays appear frequently in major periodicals.*

In the following article, Parini describes Steinbeck's early and unsuccessful college years, when he performed various duties as a ranch hand on California farms. Working closely with immigrant and itinerant laborers inspired him to later create characters such as George and Lennie in Of Mice and Men. *As Parini notes, Steinbeck was not expecting the novella to garner the immediate critical attention that it received. The book became an instant best seller and propelled Steinbeck into the role of unwilling celebrity.*

[As a college freshman, John Steinbeck] limped through his first year at Stanford, getting two 'cinch notices' [warnings from teachers of unsatisfactory performance] and missing many classes; while the subjects that he studied caught his interest, especially English composition and a literature course called 'Narration and Exposition', he generally found himself unable to keep up with the pace set by his instructors. In December, his parents were sent a letter by the Dean of Students, who warned them that their son was 'not working up to his potential'. This news . . . sent [his mother] Olive Steinbeck through the roof. 'She wanted him to do so well,' his sister recalls, 'and she just couldn't believe it when he got into trouble with the deans. She guessed he would flunk out entirely, and it made her very angry.'

Inspiration from Working the Land

Steinbeck staggered through to the end of the academic year, and that summer [his father] John Ernst got his son and his son's roommate [George Mors] temporary jobs with a surveying unit working in the Santa Lucias, near Big Sur. Mors and Steinbeck were giddy with delight, imagining a summer of relative ease in the open countryside, but the work proved rougher than they expected. The young men were forced to lug heavy surveying equipment up steep hillsides through wiry brush and prickly scrub. The food was rotten, and—according to Steinbeck—there were rattlesnakes to sidestep and poison oak to avoid. The two college boys lasted only a few weeks, when they quit in frustration. John Ernst, who always hesitated to get into any kind of fight with his son and went out of his way to smooth things over, got them easier (and lower-paying) jobs as maintenance men at the Spreckels [sugar] plant in Salinas.

Steinbeck's association with his father's old company, Spreckels, continued over the next few years, during summers and long drop-out periods. The sugar company had grown fairly large by 1920, and it owned or leased ranches all along the Salinas Valley from King City to Santa Clara; Steinbeck worked in different capacities on several of them. While cultivating beet for the sugar plant in Salinas was their major function, the ranches also raised beef cattle and, to feed the livestock, produced hay and alfalfa. Each ranch had a permanent staff, but during certain times of the year itinerant ranch-hands were hired. These were the 'bindlestiffs' who eventually became the subject of Steinbeck's *Of Mice and Men*: broken men who wandered the countryside looking for a bit of work on this or that farm. They would do anything—buck barley, feed the pigs, dig wells, harvest fruit or vegetables, mend fences.

Nothing was ever wasted on Steinbeck; he instinctively knew how to milk his experience for what it was worth in imaginative value. One can tie a huge number of characters, incidents and settings from his later fiction to early working experiences acquired during periods away from Stanford. The specific incident that sparked *Of Mice and Men* may have occurred during this time, as Steinbeck later suggested to an interviewer:

> I was a bindlestiff myself for quite a spell. I worked in the same country that the story is laid in. The characters are composites to a certain extent. Lennie was a real person. He's in an insane asylum in California right now. I worked alongside him for many weeks. He didn't kill a girl. He killed a ranch foreman. Got sore because the boss had fired his pal and stuck a pitchfork right through his stomach. I hate to tell you how many times. I saw him do it. We couldn't stop him until it was too late.

While Steinbeck may have been indulging in a bit of role-playing for the interviewer here, the vividness of his fiction about people like George and Lennie may well be tied to his firsthand experience on these ranches. 'I think John preferred those jobs to studying,' his sister says. 'He always came home full of stories, and we would sit around the kitchen table and listen for hours. I didn't believe a lot of the stories, but I didn't care. They were good stories, and they were meant to be taken as such.'

Apart from the bindlestiffs, who were mostly Anglo-Saxon in origin, Steinbeck encountered workers who had flooded in from Mexico and the Philippines in search of wages. The Mexicans, in particular, caught the young man's fancy, and they would play a central role in *Tortilla Flat*, where he evoked a number of vivid Mexican characters, such as Sweets Ramirez, one of his most endearing creations. Indeed, Mexico itself would become a favourite place for him to visit, and he would set a novella, *The Pearl*, as well as the screenplay *Viva Zapata!*, in that country. . . .

Drawing on his personal experiences with immigrant laborers, John Steinbeck found inspiration for his novel Of Mice and Men. Hulton Archive/Getty Images.

An Unexpected Success

[Many years later, when Steinbeck had completed *Of Mice and Men* in the fall of 1936, he asserted,] 'I don't expect the little book, *Of Mice and Men*, to make any money.' The reaction at the publisher was, as usual, mixed—Steinbeck had never yet written a book that everybody thought was going to do well—but [his editor] Pat Covici claimed to like it and said he would bring it out 'early in the New Year'. Steinbeck sensed no real enthusiasm from Covici, although he was grateful that his editor was willing to stand behind him.

Covici had been standing firmly behind his new author, acquiring the rights to all of Steinbeck's earlier books (*Cup of Gold*, *The Pastures of Heaven* and *To a God Unknown*) and re-launching them in new editions with prefaces. Thus far, *Tortilla Flat* was by far the most commercially viable of Steinbeck's books, and it continued to sell steadily through the summer of 1936. The hostile reaction of some critics to *In Dubious Battle* had, unquestionably, depressed its sales, but it was none the less considered by Covici 'a moderate success'. The fact that Steinbeck appeared to be endlessly productive was heartening to Covici, who foresaw a long and continuing relationship between editor and author. . . .

Of Mice and Men . . . appeared in early February 1937. The public response was swift and gratifying, taking Steinbeck's publishers and the author himself by huge surprise. By the middle of February, the book had sold 117,000 copies. 'That's a hell of a lot of books,' Steinbeck wrote to Pat Covici on 28 February, rubbing it in. He was justified in doing so; the book was flying out of the stores, and the press had begun to swarm around Steinbeck, desperate for interviews.

The reviews were mostly respectful, even complimentary, although *Time* sneered at the little novel, calling it a 'fairy tale'. Writing in *The Nation*, Mark Van Doren embodied the negative reaction to the book: 'All but one of the persons in Mr Steinbeck's extremely brief novel are subhuman if the range of the word human is understood to coincide with the range thus far established by fiction.' Ralph Thompson's review in *The New York Times* (27 February) was more typical, calling the book 'completely disarming'. Another critic, Harry Hansen, went so far as to nominate the novel 'the finest bit of prose fiction of this decade'.

A Literary Classic

Steinbeck's story of two wandering 'bindlestiffs', George and Lennie, has become a permanent fixture of American literature. The book's subject is the nature of innocence, and it is explored with extraordinary compassion and skill. The semiretarded Lennie and his guardian, George Milton, are men with a fragile dream of owning land and settling down into a paradisial future. 'Guys like us, that work on ranches, are the loneliest guys in the world. They got no family. They don't belong no place,' George tells his friend, who can barely understand him. 'With us it ain't like that. We got a future. We got somebody to talk to that gives a damn about us. . . . An' why? Because I got you to look after me, and you got me to look after you, and that's why.'

Bound by their dream of settling down together on land they can farm, George and Lennie walk together into their inevitably dim future. On the farm where the story takes place, Steinbeck's odd couple meet Candy, an ageing farmhand who grieves over his toothless, rheumatic dog, which is finally shot because it smells up the bunkhouse. They brush against the evil son of the boss, Curley, and Curley's wife, the seductive and stupid woman who is accidentally murdered by Lennie at the climax of the story. Other fine characters include Slim, a 'jerkline skinner' who has 'Godlike eyes' that fasten on to a man so firmly he can't think of anything else, and Crooks, a proudly benevolent stable buck with a hunched back who, because of his black skin, is shunned by the rest.

[Steinbeck's friend] Ed Ricketts had told Steinbeck that he should not be waylaid by what 'could' or 'should' happen but by what 'did'. It is therefore interesting that Steinbeck originally called the book 'Something That Happened'. (Ricketts, in fact, suggested the change in title.) The author remains detached throughout, blaming no one for the fact that, in Robert Burns's words, 'the best laid schemes o' mice an' men gang aft a'gley'. [Critic] Antonia Seixas has noted that 'the hardest task a writer can set himself is to tell a story of "something that happened" without explaining "why"—and make it convincing and moving". This, indeed, is what Steinbeck accomplishes in this brief, compelling novella (or novelette, as short novels were often called in the Thirties).

We do, however, get something like moral reflection from Slim, the most intelligent character in the story. He is a man 'whose ear heard more than was said to him', and he listens to George tell of the dream he shares with Lennie with rueful detachment. He alone realizes that the dream will necessarily fail; the economies of their situation will not allow for success. It is Slim, whom Steinbeck calls the 'prince of the ranch', who tells George in the final poignant scene that he had to act directly in response to Lennie's unfortunate killing of Curley's wife. 'You hadda, George', he tells him in the end, after George has killed his best friend humanely to save him from being lynched, 'you hadda.' That Slim is controlling the action is signalled by his invitation to George at the end to come and have a drink with him: 'Come on, George. Me an' you'll go in an' get a drink.' George agrees and is led up to the highway by Slim.

The novella showed a side of American life that most people had never experienced directly, and Steinbeck's plain style struck readers then, as it still does, as true and memorable. As simple narrative, *Of Mice and Men* demonstrates once again the raw storytelling power Steinbeck could summon, and the final scene, which teeters on the brink of sentimentality, seems both inevitable and deeply tragic. One grieves, with George, for Lennie.

But there are many other layers in this book. For a start, it can be read as sharp protest; the mere fact that Steinbeck describes so concretely the situation of bindlestiffs in California was a political act in the charged atmosphere of the late Thirties. The author's urgency, his anger at the way men like George and Lennie were being treated, is felt on every page.

One might also find various allegorical strands in the text; its mythlike simplicity invites this kind of interpretation. Finally as the fruit of Steinbeck's inquiry into 'non-teleological thinking',[1] *Of Mice and Men* may be considered an accomplished piece of speculative fiction, as [critic] Peter Lisca has pointed out.

Steinbeck on Stage and in the Public Eye

The fact that *Of Mice and Men* was conceived as a play in novella form made it easily convertible for the stage, and it was not long before Steinbeck was engaged by George S. Kaufman, the Broadway playwright and director, to produce a version for the footlights. (Sam H. Harris, who was much revered on Broadway, was enlisted as producer, thus ensuring a first-class production.) Kaufman wrote to encourage Steinbeck, telling him that his novel 'drops almost naturally into play form and no one knows that better than you'. He added, 'It is only the second act that seems to me to need fresh invention. You have the two natural scenes for it—bunkhouse and the negro's room, but I think the girl should come into both these scenes, and that the fight between Lennie and Curley, which will climax Act 2, must be over the girl. I think the girl should have a scene with Lennie *before* the scene in which he kills her. The girl, I think, should be drawn more fully: she is the motivating force of the whole thing and should loom larger.' (The fact that she was never even given a name shows that Steinbeck did not intend her to play a large part in the story. As Kaufman wished, her role was greatly expanded for the play and, later, for the film.)

Meanwhile, *Of Mice and Men* leaped on to the bestseller lists. Letters to Steinbeck poured in from strangers and friends alike, as did requests for interviews, readings, public appear-

---

1. In *The Sea of Cortez*, Steinbeck and Ed Ricketts explained that non-teleological thinking "concerns itself primarily not with what should be, or could be, or might be, but rather with what actually 'is'" attempting to answer the "questions *what* or *how*, instead of *why*."

ances and autographs. To his chagrin, Steinbeck was often forced to travel several miles to the nearest telephone to respond to urgent requests of one kind or another, most of which proved mere annoyances. Once, a tourist turned up at his front gate with her little daughter in tow, and when she saw Steinbeck she cried, 'Dance for the man, darling! Dance!' To Elizabeth Otis, the frustrated Steinbeck wrote, 'This ballyhoo is driving me nuts.'

For some time [Steinbeck and his wife, Carol,] had been hoping to visit Europe, and they had now both the money and a good reason to get out of the country. They boarded a freighter called *The Sagebrush* from San Francisco to the East Coast on 23 March, via the Panama Canal. . . . The ship docked in Philadelphia, and the Steinbecks took a train into New York's Pennsylvania Station, where they were met by Pat Covici, eager to waylay his newly famous author for a couple of weeks. . . .

[Steinbeck] found himself in a bind that would become only too familiar. His growing reputation had turned him, suddenly, into a public person, but his shyness and essential disbelief in publicity and 'society' tugged him in the opposite direction. 'He was never happy at parties,' Elaine Steinbeck says. 'Never in his life. And he always detested public events. He would much rather stay home and read, or write or talk to friends. Publicity always depressed him.'

The Social Environment in *Of Mice and Men*

Joyce Moss and George Wilson

In the following selection, the authors examine the historical context of Of Mice and Men. *During the Great Depression, when the novella takes place, America's migrant farmers struggled to make a living while being underpaid, underfed, and underemployed. Itinerant workers lived their migratory lives at the mercy of the seasonal labor demands of the farmers. As unskilled workers, they were rarely represented by unions, and when they did strike for better wages or working conditions, they became victims of vigilante violence. The plight of these men engaged John Steinbeck's imagination at a time when he was becoming more interested in California's social and economic problems.*

During the late 1930s, California was struggling not only with the economic problems of the Great Depression, but also with severe labor strife. Labor conflicts occurred on the docks and packing sheds and fields. [John] Steinbeck wrote movingly about the struggles of migrant farm workers in three successive novels: *In Dubious Battle* (1936), *Of Mice and Men* (1937), and *The Grapes of Wrath* (1939). Agriculture as a working-culture was undergoing a historic change. In 1938, about half the nation's grain was harvested by mechanical combines that enabled five men to do the work that had previously required 350. Only a short time before, thousands of itinerant single men had roamed the western states following the harvests. Their labor had been essential to the success of the large farms. By 1900, about 125,000 migrants travelled along a route from Minnesota west to Washington state. Many traveled by rail in the empty boxcars that were later used to transport grain. At the turn of the century, the men were paid an average of $2.50 to $3 a day, plus room and board. The "room" was often a tent.

A Migratory Life

Wages had risen somewhat at the time of World War I, partly because of the Industrial Workers of the World, which established an 800-mile picket line across the Great Plains states. The "habitual" workers lived the migratory life for years until they grew too old to work. By the late 1930s there were an estimated 200,000 to 350,000 migrants: underpaid, underfed, and underemployed. The migrant worker was always partially unemployed, the nature of the occupation making his work seasonal. The maximum a worker could make was $400 a year, with the average about $300. Yet California's agricultural system could not exist without the migrant workers. It was a problem that would continue for decades. The farms in the state were more like food factories, the "farmers" were absentee owners, remaining in their city offices and hiring local managers to oversee the farming. In short, California's agriculture was not "farming" in the traditional sense. It was an industry like the lumber and oil industries. At the end of the 1930s, one-third of all large-scale farms in the United States were in California, reflecting the trend toward corporate farming. These farms had greatly fluctuating labor demands, and owners encouraged heavy immigration of low-wage foreign workers, usually Chinese, Japanese, and Filipinos. Mexicans began arriving in large numbers around 1910 and represented the largest percentage of the migrant workforce for about twenty years.

During these years, there were thousands of white Americans among the migrants, usually single men who followed the harvesting. Steinbeck writes about them in *Of Mice and*

Men. These "bindle-stiffs," as they were known, had no union representation for several reasons. They had no money to pay dues, and they moved from location to location so often that it was difficult to organize them. In addition, American unionism, with its traditional craft setup, did not welcome unskilled workers like farm laborers. In 1930, the Cannery and Agricultural Workers Industrial Union, a Communist-led union, organized the first effective drive among the migrants. During 1933, the group followed the migrants and harvests, organizing a nine-county cotton pickers' strike that affected 12,000 workers. By mid-1934, the union had led about fifty strikes involving 50,000 workers. The group's leaders claimed to have a membership of 21,000 and said they had raised the basic hourly field wage from an average of 15 cents to 17.5 cents an hour in 1932 to an average of 27.5 cents in 1934.

California Growers Needed Migrant Workers

In the summer of 1934, the union was broken up by the anti-Communist activities of employers and state authorities. Its last stand was at an apricot pickers' strike in June 1934. Deputies herded 200 strikers into a cattle pen, arrested some of the leaders, and transported the rest of the strikers out of the county. In trials, the union's president and secretary and six of their associates were convicted of treason. Five of the eight prisoners were later paroled and the other three were freed when an appellate court reversed the convictions in 1937. The existence of a strike was the greatest threat to California's growers. The harvest couldn't wait while negotiations dragged on. Crops had to be picked within a few days of ripening or the result would be financial ruin. This situation created much social unrest. In the 1930s, vigilante activity against strikers and organizers was bloody. Many workers, as well as a number of strike breakers and townspeople, were injured. Vigilantism was not uncommon in early union activities, but in

California's farming industry it was particularly vicious, which was odd because the growers could not have existed without the migrants' labor. During peak seasonal demand, growers hired as many as 175,000 workers.

Yet after the harvests most of these workers were not needed. Growers argued that they could not be responsible for paying workers year-round when they were needed only for a few weeks or months. Steady work was impossible not only because of the seasonal nature of the industry but also because jobs were widely separated and time was lost traveling on the road. Steinbeck wrote *Of Mice and Men* at a time when he was becoming involved in California's social and economic problems. In the novel, he wrote about a group of people, the white male migrant workers, who were to shortly disappear from American culture. World War II absorbed many of the workers in the war effort in the 1940s. Although farm workers were generally exempt from the draft, the expansion of the defense industries to supply the U.S. military needs reduced the pool of surplus labor. The novel's continued popularity over the decades clearly shows that it has transcended its historical times.

Of Mice and Men and the American Dream

Characters in *Of Mice and Men* Search for the Promise of America

Kenneth D. Swan

Kenneth D. Swan is a John Steinbeck scholar who has served as an editor for the Steinbeck Quarterly *and the Steinbeck Monograph Series. He coordinated the Taylor University–Ball State University Bicentennial Steinbeck Seminar in 1976, and since then his essays on Steinbeck have been widely anthologized.*

In the following essay, Swan enumerates the ways in which Steinbeck explores the American scene in his various works. In Of Mice and Men *in particular, Swan says that Steinbeck depicts an America in which dreams are too idealistic to be realized and in which people are inextricably related to the land. Ultimately, Swan argues, Steinbeck's novels show America as a place of constant change, against which his characters must continually struggle.*

What was America like to John Steinbeck? Or phrased another way, what is it like to be a human being and live in America in the twentieth century? This question in a very significant way seems to be the focus of much of Steinbeck's fiction. As much as anything, Steinbeck, as a writer, was a first-rate interpreter of the American scene. The Swedish Academy in announcing the Nobel Prize award stated of John Steinbeck, "He possesses an unbiased instinct for America, be it good or bad." . . .

[In the] fiction of John Steinbeck which explores the American scene, we see many of the characters in search of

Kenneth D. Swan, "John Steinbeck in Search of America," in *Steinbeck's Prophetic Vision of America: Proceedings of the Taylor University-Ball State University Bicentennial Steinbeck Seminar*, ed. Tetsumaro Hayashi and Kenneth D. Swan. Taylor University, 1976. Copyright © 1976 Tetsumaro Hayashi and Kenneth D. Swan. Reproduced by permission of copyright owner, Dr. Tetsumaro Hayashi/Ball State University-sponsored Steinbeck Society of America projects (1968–93).

what America promises but caught in the clutches of circumstances which often seem to frustrate their search. First, we see in the writings of John Steinbeck America as a place where too often the minority is oppressed by the value system of the majority middle class materialistic culture. Examine *The Pastures of Heaven, Tortilla Flat, In Dubious Battle, The Grapes of Wrath,* or many of Steinbeck's short stories. Second, we see America as a place which spawns dreams and wishes which are sometimes too visionary or idealistic to be realized. Consider *The Pastures of Heaven, In Dubious Battle, Of Mice and Men,* and, symbolically consider *The Short Reign of Pippin IV.* Third, we see America as a place where freedom, equality, and human dignity are promised, but are only guaranteed through effort, insistence, and proper insight. Read *In Dubious Battle, The Grapes of Wrath, East of Eden,* and by analogy, consider *The Moon Is Down.* Fourth, we see America as a place of conflicting value systems—a pluralistic people trying to live together. Observe *To a God Unknown, In Dubious Battle, The Grapes of Wrath, Cannery Row,* and *The Wayward Bus.* Fifth, we see America as a place where people tackle problems, experiment, make many mistakes, but continue to seek better answers and alternatives. Read *In Dubious Battle, The Grapes of Wrath,* and *East of Eden.* Sixth, we see America as a place where people, like people the world over, continue to struggle with universal problems, moral questions, and ethical dilemmas. Consider almost any one of Steinbeck's books but especially *To a God Unknown, The Grapes of Wrath, East of Eden,* and *The Winter of Our Discontent.* Seventh, we see America as a place where people and land are inextricably related, sometimes economically and materially but often spiritually. Read *To a God Unknown, In Dubious Battle, Of Mice and Men,* and *The Grapes of Wrath.* Yet too often the land and its resources are wasted, misused, and exploited. Observe Steinbeck's comments in *Travels with Charley in Search of America* and *America and Americans.*

In this scene from the Interlochen Arts Academy production of the play Of Mice and Men, *Lennie (Paul Schierhorn) accidentally kills Curley's wife (Pat Dermody) by hugging her to death with excess affection. John Steinbeck's novel,* Of Mice and Men, *illustrates the destructive aspects of American society and the impossibility of the American dream.* Henry Groskinsky/Time & Life Pictures/Getty Images.

A Place of Constant Change

Last, as much as anything, we see in Steinbeck's writings, America as a place of constant change. Look at any of his books and you see people struggling with change, trying to maintain freedom, dignity, and value in the face of change. With the past giving way to the present and becoming merely a memory, and with the reality of the present being pushed aside for the promise of the future, how can the American people, in the face of such change, stay the same? John Steinbeck's answer is they can't, but they can in new circumstances perceive the value of human worth, the possibility of facing reality and solving problems, and the spiritual identity of man to man.

In conclusion, in the final paragraph of [*America and Americans*], the final book which Steinbeck published two years before his death, Steinbeck considers the future of

America. He says, ". . . the fascinating unknown is everywhere. How will the Americans act and react to a new set of circumstances for which new rules must be made? We know from our past some of the things we will do. We will make many mistakes; we always have. We are in the perplexing period of change. We seem to be running in all directions at once—but we are running. And I believe that our history, our experience in America, has endowed us for the change that is coming."

Of Mice and Men
Describes Just One Phase
of the American Dream

Frederic I. Carpenter

Frederic I. Carpenter is the author of American Literature and
the Dream. *His scholarly essays on John Steinbeck appeared in
journals including* Southwest Review *and* Western American
Literature.

*In the following essay, Carpenter argues that Steinbeck's works
describe successive phases of the American dream.* Of Mice and
Men *illustrates an individualistic struggle to attain the American dream in its simplest form. The characters become heroic,
Carpenter says, because they refuse to deny their dream. They
also achieve an inner integrity in their unselfish willingness to
band together. In the end, however, Carpenter asserts that George
and Lennie remain only dreamers. They do not possess what he
calls "the pragmatic 'intelligence'" to fully realize their dream.*

Steinbeck's writing shows a steady progression of subject, of
thought, and of technique. Chronologically, his stories describe the pageant of the American West. From *Cup of Gold*,
which dealt with the early pirates of Panama, to the contemporary epic of the Okies [in *The Grapes of Wrath*], they have
their background in history. First the Spaniards and Indians,
then the American homesteaders, then the *paisano* descen-
dants of the Spaniards and Indians, then the Communist agi-
tators, and now the depression migrants—all have lived, actually.

But beyond history, these novels illustrate the logical development of an idea: they describe successive phases of the

Frederick I. Carpenter, "John Steinbeck: American Dreamer," *Southwest Review*, vol.
24, no. 4, Summer 1941, pp. 454–67.

American dream. First the dream of conquest, then of escape, then of settlement and ownership. But something was lacking in all these early dreams—some possessive egotism vitiated them. The novels of Steinbeck's second period describe more unselfish types of Americans, who fail for other reasons: irresponsibility, or fanaticism, or defective mentality. Most recently, *The Long Valley* and *The Grapes of Wrath* have suggested the possible realization of the American dream through courage and active intelligence.

Finally, Steinbeck has gradually developed an artistic technique for describing dreamers. His first three novels failed through lack of objective reality: the earliest described pirates as if they were dreamers; the second described dreamers without explaining their motivation; the third mystically merged characters and author in a confused symbolism. But his mature novels succeeded because they described dreamers objectively, and made clear their motivation; the creator separated himself from his creatures. These characters remained insignificant in so far as they remained dreamers, merely. In his later short stories and in *The Grapes of Wrath* Steinbeck's characters have integrated dream with action and have lived on both levels, independently of their author....

The Old American Dream

Of Mice and Men describes the individualistic survival of the old American dream. Constantly repeated, because it is common to all Americans, this dream gives significance to a story of outcasts and failures: "Just like heaven. Ever'body wants a little piece of lan'.... Nobody never gets to heaven, and nobody gets no land. It's just in their head. They're all the time talkin' about it, but it's jus' in their head." Security, independence, a piece of land, the pioneer's dream and once almost the American reality; but now it's "just in their head." This is the American tragedy.

But why an imbecile for a hero? Why a [Negro], a cripple, and a moron for supporting cast? It has been said that this story is not tragic, because its characters lack significance. But I think the story is tragic, although it is not primarily a tragedy of character. It is a tragedy of idea. These "heroes" achieve significance because they give expression to the American dream in its simplest form. They become heroic, because they refuse to deny their dream. George says, "Guys like us got no fambly. They make a little stake an' then they blow it in. They ain't got nobody in the worl' that gives a hoot in hell about 'em—." They refute the despair of [poet] Vachel Lindsay:

Not that they starve, but starve so dream-
lessly,

Not that they sow, but that they seldom
reap,

Not that they serve, but have no gods to
serve,

Not that they die, but that they die like
sheep.

Serving an unknown God, they do not die like sheep:

George was quiet for a moment. "But not us," he said.

"Because—"

"Because I got you an'—"

"An' I got you. We got each other, that's what, that gives a hoot in hell about us," Lennie cried in triumph.

And so they die in triumph with their dream.

In this novel the dream which has dominated Steinbeck's thought from the beginning reaches its final phase. George and Lennie express what is best in it. Unlike Henry Morgan [in *Cup of Gold*] who was "not very intelligent" because he was utterly selfish, these poor men see beyond themselves. Like the Joad family [in *The Grapes of Wrath*], these native Americans seek unselfishly to band together. George becomes a responsible leader, and the others share. If they are doomed, it is not because of what is false within—they have achieved inner integrity. They lack only the pragmatic "intelligence" necessary to bring the dream to realization. Because they lack that, they remain dreamers merely: at the end George gets drunk and tries to forget.

Of Mice and Men Offers a Pessimistic View of the American Dream

Duncan Reith

When this essay was published, Duncan Reith was teaching English at the Thomas Hardye School in Dorchester, England.

In the following selection, Reith contends that John Steinbeck's symbolic descriptions in the opening scenes of Of Mice and Men *foreshadow the lonely and bleak experiences of the characters. The novella captures the extremely difficult working and living conditions of California migrant workers in the early twentieth century. Their lives, Reith says, were shaped by inescapable hierarchies and discriminatory practices inherent in the farms on which they labored. Thus, men like George and Lennie could only gain a sense of power in their dreams. Even when they are shown a glimpse of progress toward their American dream, something inevitably happens to snatch away those hopes of a better future. Reith concludes that while these characters strive toward self-sufficiency, Steinbeck's final message is that dreams that exist in a culture of brutality and exploitation of the weak are doomed to fail.*

Albert Bierstadt's 'Mount Corcoran' (1878), an enormous, romantic vision of the Sierra Nevada, is perhaps the most well-known painting of the Californian landscape. In the background, golden foothills lead away from the green pool up to a dreamy profusion of heavenly clouds. In the foreground, by contrast, we are offered precise, realistic details: a clutch of trees, one fallen trunk in the river, perhaps the debris of the winter's flooding. A solitary bear, dwarfed by the sweeping, dramatic landscape, comes to test the water.

Duncan Reith, "Futile Dreams and Stagnation: Politics in 'Of Mice and Men,'" *The English Review*, vol. 15, November 2004, pp. 6–9. Copyright © 2004 Philip Allan Updates. Reproduced by permission of Philip Allan Updates.

A Predatory World

Steinbeck opens *Of Mice and Men* with a similar set of symbols. Lennie Small is described as a bear, huge and strong yet somehow insignificant when framed against such an imposing landscape. His green pool is a stagnant Soledad (the ranch on which he and his friend George find work) and the ripples he causes there come back to him. His progression from killing mouse to dog to woman ends predictably in his own death. At the end, Lennie gazes longingly at the Gabilan mountains and George sends him to that heaven with a gun.

Steinbeck marks the near side of his river with images of hell and decay. Animals balance the need to drink with the need to avoid predators. In the river itself, there is suggestive activity. A carp tries to come up for air but is drawn mysteriously back down into the dark water. A heron waits in the shadows. Later, its head lances down, plucks out and swallows a water snake.

This symbolic scene lets the reader know what to expect. Events in the river will be mirrored by events on the ranch. For example, when Curley's wife meets her fate, a four-taloned Jackson fork is suspended above her, and her body flops 'like a fish'. The message is clear: ranch life will be a lonely experience, as the word Soledad [Spanish for "solitude"] suggests. Men live like animals, in a pecking order, struggling for survival, growing old and weak, helpless individuals in a predatory world which will determine their fate. The only escape from this bleak predicament is to a land of dreams.

Hard Times

Films of *Of Mice and Men* rarely do justice to Steinbeck's depiction of the bleak existence endured by migrant ranch hands. Sanitised for the average American cinema audience, the story usually becomes a trite tale of strong friendship in the face of mild adversity. The most recent Hollywood offering ends with Gary Sinise and John Malkovich as George and Lennie strolling together through golden fields in a celebration of the spiritual benefits of working the land. Throughout, the characters have worn stylish clothing which changes in each scene. It would be hard to imagine a greater distortion of the ranch hand's experience.

These were hard times. In the middle of the Great Depression, the influx of a million migrants into California from the Dustbowl states had made labour even cheaper, and competition for jobs was fierce. The wealthy landowners could pick and choose a workforce, and offer low wages, because the ranch hands were in no position to complain. Indeed, George and Lennie would be thankful for the work when most Oklahoma migrants, like the Joad family in *The Grapes of Wrath*, were utterly destitute and enduring barbaric conditions and oppression in overcrowded camps. Even local ranch hands like George and Lennie lived in very basic accommodation with only the barest essentials. They worked all day in the hot sun until their skin was almost black. Utterly dependent on the boss for their welfare and sustenance, they could be 'canned' at any moment. With low pay and no security, they could not make long-term plans, and could not afford to start families. All the ranch workers in the novel remain single, wasting what little money they can set aside in the local 'cathouse'. In the context of this social and economic background, their dreams of living 'off the fatta the lan'' are both psychologically necessary and ludicrously far-fetched.

The best laid schemes o' mice and men

Gang aft agley

And lea'e us nought but grief and pain

For promised joy.

The novel's title, taken from Robert Burns's poem 'To a Mouse' (1785), invites the reader to make comparisons with the plight of the tenant farmers in Scotland in the late eighteenth century. In the poem, the tenant farmer, dependent on an absentee landlord for food and shelter and knowing he could be evicted on the instant, feels as powerless as the mouse whose house his plough has accidentally overturned. Higher rents, consolidation of farms and the introduction of large-scale commercial sheep farming to a struggling economy made the tenant farmer's position impossible and culminated in mass migration following the Highland Clearances. Steinbeck carries the same metaphor to his novel, where the mouse is a cipher for the powerless ranch hand, trapped in the pocket of a man who has no control over his own power and who cannot help but crush him.

Inescapable Hierarchies

Though Burns's poem may be read as a cry for revolution, it is difficult to read *Of Mice and Men* in the same way, for its power structures are not offered as something dispensable. At no point are we invited to believe that the brutal hierarchy could be replaced with a communist utopia and all would be well. The colour red is presented as an attractive but dangerous, and ultimately fatal, temptation. *Of Mice and Men* is no crude polemic, advocating a communist ideal. Instead, the divisions of power seem ingrained. The characters are realistic precisely because each is driven by his own will to power. Slim's authority, Carlson's brutality, Lennie's strength, Curley's posturing—each character has his own means of trying to gain influence over others. This is specifically rendered in the description of each character's hands: the temple dancer, the stick-like wrist, the bear paws, the glove fulla Vaseline.

Those who fail to achieve any influence restore their self-esteem in their imagination: in their dreams they are powerful. Thus the alternative societies offered in the text, such as Lennie and George's dream of owning a ranch, are just as hierarchical as the Soledad ranch. Even the weak characters in the pecking order inherit the brutality of the regime they have had to endure. Crooks's face lights up with pleasure in his torture of Lennie, and Candy pauses in relish of the memory of Smitty almost beating Crooks to death.

The divisions of power are permanent and meticulously observed. Characters only enter and leave the room in the order of status, a status defined by the cards which George turns in his endless game of solitaire. Each scene records the struggle and failure of each character to change that status. Curley challenges Lennie only to have his hand crushed; Crooks stands up to Curley's wife only to retreat into the 'terrible protective dignity of the negro' when he is told she could have him 'strung up so easy it aint funny'.

The rigidity of the existing hierarchy is reinforced by the ideology of the ranch hands themselves. The Western magazines that they 'secretly believe' contain tales of solitary individuals somehow capable of extraordinary feats of skill which set them apart from their fellow men. Slim is initially presented to us as the embodiment of this fantasy, an archetypal cowboy capable of 'killing a fly on the wheeler's butt without touching the mule', although we are later allowed to see through the facade: we note, for example, his shaking hands when he fails to intervene in the killing of Candy's dog.

The Western magazines show the ranch hands a world of gunmanship, posses and retributive justice. However, this culture is applied on the ranch by characters struggling to satisfy their will to power, and what emerges is not justice but a vengeful brutality. Curley's wife threatens to have Crooks lynched, Carlson shoots Candy's dog merely because of its smell, and Curley hunts Lennie down not to achieve justice for the killing of his wife but because Lennie has crushed his hand.

A Glimpse of a Better World

The harsh economic conditions and the self-centred application of Western magazine culture combine to create a world which discriminates for disability, gender and race. The disabled characters like Candy become old and useless with no place to go and no future. Women are treated as prostitutes. Curley's wife is denied the dignity of a name, and is described as a tart and a lulu, the same name given to Slim's dog. The negro Crooks is housed with the animals, and suffers in abject loneliness. The ranch his father owned has long ago been taken away, and the mauled copy of the California Civil Code of 1905 on his shelf suggests many vain years of trying to recover it.

Yet at the edges of this desperate gloom, Steinbeck allows us glimpses of a better world. The ranch hands play a horseshoe game in which Crooks is allowed to participate, and the contrived puns on stake and tenement here suggest the possibility of holding property in common. George has progressed from an attitude in the past in Sacramento when he exploited and ridiculed Lennie to a parental role in which he now cares for him. The novel closes with a distinction between those like Carlson and Curley who will never understand the emotions and needs of others, and those like George and Slim who are capable of understanding and forming friendships but who have to cope with a society so sickened by the struggle to survive that they are forced into mercy killing. Thus the glimmer of hope for a better world is violently extinguished.

Of Mice and Men argues that the gulf between the gritty struggle for survival and the ideal dream life can never be bridged, except in death. While Steinbeck exposes the inequalities in society and encourages the reader to sympathise with the plight of poor migrant workers, his depiction of the inherent will to power in human nature shows us that attempts to change the social system will be futile. As the opening scene reminds us, men are trapped in a set of relations which work like fate. Americans will continue to dream, like Martin Luther King, that the nation will live out the true meaning of its creed, that all men are created equal. But for

Steinbeck the American Dream of self-sufficiency and living off the fat of the land, premised as it is on a gun culture which involves brutality and the exploitation of the weak, is doomed to failure. The magnitude of this failure is recorded by the extent to which Lennie, a cipher for America, is denied life, liberty and the pursuit of happiness.

The American Eden in *Of Mice and Men* Is an Illusion

Louis Owens

A revered John Steinbeck critic, the late Louis Owens was professor of English at the University of California, Davis. His books include John Steinbeck's Re-Vision of America *and* The Grapes of Wrath: Trouble in the Promised Land.

Owens argues in the following article that Steinbeck's use of the idyllic setting of the California Salinas Valley provides him with a symbolic landscape for exposing the flaws of an American Eden. In Of Mice and Men *Steinbeck proves that this Eden-like view of the American dream is an illusion. As Owens notes, some critics describe the novella's characters as the biblical "sons of Cain," forced to live lives of loneliness and alienation. While many critics agree that the novella strikes a tone of pessimism, Owens senses a note of hope in Lennie and his search for the perfect garden. Lennie is not a loner, and he is bolstered in his dreams by the unfailing commitment of George. Even though the dream of an American Eden seemingly dies with Lennie, Owens argues that because George has demonstrated man's commitment to man, the dream will reemerge in the future.*

The Salinas Valley imprinted itself deeply upon the consciousness of John Steinbeck, so deeply that the valley setting came to dominate his fiction and to shape his vision of America. The long, amazingly fertile Salinas Valley, with its alternately rampaging and disappearing river and its shifting, wind-driven soils, epitomized the ambiguous Eden that Steinbeck felt at the heart of the American Dream. That the valley lay close up against a dark range of mountains marking the western edge of the continent could only make this westering, Edenic quality more unmistakable and intense. If Eden were not to be found here at the fertile farthest extent of the westward trek, surely it was not to be found at all. And thus Steinbeck's valleys, large and small, became studied Edens wracked by doubt and human weakness. In these valleys Steinbeck examines, probes, tests the Eden myth, putting it under the biologist's microscope and understanding it for the illusion it is. Steinbeck searches out and exposes within his valleys the fatal flaws of the American Eden.

It was the valley setting, with the emotionally charged Eden theme and complex of symbols which it evoked, that provided the soil for Steinbeck's greatest fiction. In the ironic Edens of Steinbeck's valleys flowered the psychologically penetrating stories of *The Pastures of Heaven*, the mature craftsmanship of *In Dubious Battle* and *Of Mice and Men*, the deft precision of some of the stories in *The Long Valley*, and the crowning achievement of *The Grapes of Wrath*; and out of the intricate complexity of Steinbeck's feelings for the valley of his birth and for California's place in American thought grew the ponderously ambitious, confused, and disappointing summing-up: *East of Eden....*

The Dream of Commitment

The Eden myth looms large in *Of Mice and Men* (1937), the play-novella set *along the Salinas River* "a few miles south of Soledad." And, as in all of Steinbeck's California fiction, setting plays a central role in determining the major themes of this work. The fact that the setting for *Of Mice and Men* is a California valley dictates, according to the symbolism of Steinbeck's landscapes, that this story will take place in a fallen world and that the quest for the illusive and illusory American Eden will be of central thematic significance. In no other work does Steinbeck demonstrate greater skill in merging the real setting of his native country with the thematic structure of his novel.

Critics have consistently recognized in Lennie's dream of living "off the fatta the lan'" on a little farm the American dream of a new Eden. [Critic] Joseph Fontenrose states concisely, "The central image is the earthly paradise. . . . It is a vision of Eden." [Scholar] Peter Lisca takes this perception further, noting that "the world of *Of Mice and Men* is a fallen one, inhabited by sons of Cain, forever exiled from Eden, the little farm of which they dream." There are no Edens in Steinbeck's writing, only illusions of Eden, and in the fallen world of the Salinas Valley—which Steinbeck would later place "east of Eden"—the Promised Land is an illusory and painful dream. In this land populated by "sons of Cain," men condemned to wander in solitude, the predominant theme is that of loneliness, or what [critic] Donald Pizer has called "fear of apartness." Pizer has, in fact, discovered *the* major theme of this novel when he says, "One of the themes of *Of Mice and Men* is that men fear loneliness, that they need someone to be with and to talk to who will offer understanding and companionship."

The setting Steinbeck chose for this story brilliantly underscores the theme of man's isolation and need for commitment. Soledad is a very real, dusty little town on the western edge of the Salinas River midway down the Salinas Valley. Like most of the settings in Steinbeck's fiction, this place exists, it *is*. However, with his acute sensitivity to place names, and his knowledge of Spanish, Steinbeck was undoubtedly aware that "Soledad" translates into English as "solitude" or "loneliness." In this country of solitude and loneliness, George and Lennie stand out sharply because they have each other or, as George says, "We got somebody to talk to that gives a damn about us." Cain's question is the question again at the heart of this novel: "Am I my brother's keeper?" And the answer found in the relationship between George and Lennie is an unmistakable confirmation.

Of Mice and Men is most often read as one of Steinbeck's most pessimistic works, smacking of pessimistic determinism. Fontenrose suggests that the novel is about "the vanity of human wishes" and asserts that, more pessimistically than [the Scots poet from whose poem Steinbeck titled this novella, Robert] Burns, Steinbeck reads, "*All* schemes o' mice and men gan *ever* agley'" [my italics]. Howard Levant, in a very critical reading of the novel, concurs, declaring that "the central theme is stated and restated—the good life is impossible because humanity is flawed." In spite of the general critical reaction, and without disputing the contention that Steinbeck allows no serious hope that George and Lennie will ever achieve their dream farm, it is nonetheless possible to read *Of Mice and Men* in a more optimistic light than has been customary. In previous works we have seen a pattern established in which the Steinbeck hero achieves greatness in the midst of, even because of, apparent defeat. In *Of Mice and Men*, Steinbeck accepts, very non-teleologically,[1] the fact that man is flawed and the Eden myth mere illusion. However, critics have consistently under-valued Steinbeck's emphasis on the theme of commitment, which runs through the novel and which is the chief ingredient in the creation of the Steinbeck hero.

The dream of George and Lennie represents a desire to defy the curse of Cain and fallen man—to break the curse pattern of wandering and loneliness imposed on the outcasts and to return to the perfect garden. George and Lennie achieve all of this dream that is possible in the real world: they are their brother's keeper. Unlike the solitary Cain and the solitary men who inhabit the novel, they have someone who cares. The dream of the farm merely symbolizes their deep mutual commitment, a commitment that is immediately sensed by the other characters in the novel. The ranch owner is suspicious of the relationship, protesting, "I never seen one guy

1. Steinbeck and his friend Ed Ricketts explained that non-teleological thinking "concerns itself primarily not with what should be, or could be, or might be, but rather with what actually 'is.'"

take so much trouble for another guy." Slim, the godlike jerk-line skinner, admires the relationship and says, "Ain't many guys travel around together. . . . I don't know why. Maybe everybody in the whole damn world is scared of each other." Candy, the one-handed swamper, and Crooks, the deformed black stablehand, also sense the unique commitment between the two laborers, and in their moment of unity Candy and Crooks turn as one to defend Lennie from the threat posed by Curley's wife. The influence of George and Lennie's mutual commitment, and of their dream, has for an instant made these crippled sons of Cain their brother's keepers and broken the grip of loneliness and solitude in which they exist. Lennie's yearning for the rabbits and for all soft, living things symbolizes the yearning all men have for warm, living contact. It is this yearning, described by Steinbeck as "the inarticulate and powerful yearning of all men," which makes George need Lennie just as much as Lennie needs George and which sends Curley's wife wandering despairingly about the ranch in search of companionship. Whereas Fontenrose has suggested that "the individualistic desire for carefree enjoyment of pleasures is the serpent in the garden" in this book, the real serpent is loneliness and the barriers between men and between men and women that create and reinforce this loneliness.

Lennie as Imperfection in Humanity

Lennie has been seen as representing "the frail nature of primeval innocence" and as the id to George's ego or the body to George's brain. In the novel, *Lennie* is repeatedly associated with animals or described as childlike. He appears in the opening scene dragging his feet "the way a bear drags his paws," and in the final scene he enters the clearing in the brush "as silently as a creeping bear." Slim says of Lennie, "He's jes' like a kid, ain't he," and George repeats, "Sure, he's jes' like a kid." The unavoidable truth is, however, that Lennie, be he innocent "natural," uncontrollable id, or simply a huge

The Salinas Valley in California provides an idyllic setting for John Steinbeck's novel Of Mice and Men. *Steinbeck uses this Eden-like landscape to expose the flaws of the American dream.* George Rose/Getty Images.

child, is above all dangerous. Unlike Benjy in [William Faulkner's] *The Sound and the Fury* (whom Steinbeck may have had in mind when describing the incident in Weed in which Lennie clings bewildered to the girl's dress), Lennie is monstrously powerful and has a propensity for killing things. Even if Lennie had not killed Curley's wife, he would sooner or later have done something fatal to bring violence upon himself, as the lynch mob that hunted him in Weed suggests.

Steinbeck's original title for *Of Mice and Men* was "Something That Happened," a title suggesting that Steinbeck was taking a purely non-teleological or nonblaming point of view in this novel. If we look at the novel in this way, it becomes clear that Lennie dies because he has been created incapable of dealing with society and is, in fact, a menace to society. Like Pepé in "Flight," Tularecito in *The Pastures of Heaven*, and Frankie in *Cannery Row*, Lennie is a "natural" who loses when he is forced to confront society. This is simply the way it is— something that happened—and when George kills Lennie he is not only saving him from the savagery of the pursuers, he is, as [critic] John Ditsky says, acknowledging that "Lennie's situation is quite hopeless." Ditsky further suggests that Lennie's death represents "a matter of cold hard necessity imposing itself upon the frail hopes of man." Along these same lines, [critic] Joan Steele declares that "Lennie has to be destroyed because he is a 'loner' whose weakness precludes his cooperating with George and hence working constructively toward their mutual goal." Lennie, however, is not a 'loner'; it is, in fact, the opposite, overwhelming and uncontrollable urge for contact that brings about Lennie's destruction and the destruction of living creatures he comes into contact with. Nonetheless, Steele makes an important point when she suggests that because of Lennie the dream of the Edenic farm was never a possibility. Lennie's flaw represents the inherent imperfection in humanity that renders Eden forever an impossibility. Lennie would have brought his imperfection with him to the little farm, and he would have killed the rabbits.

When Lennie dies, the teleological dream of the Edenic farm dies with him, for while Lennie's weakness doomed the dream it was only his innocence that kept it alive. The death of the dream, however, does not force *Of Mice and Men* to end on the strong note of pessimism critics have consistently claimed. For while the dream of the farm perishes, the theme of commitment achieves its strongest statement in the book's conclusion. Unlike Candy, who abandons responsibility for his old dog and allows Carlson to shoot him, George remains his brother's keeper without faltering even to the point of killing Lennie while Lennie sees visions of Eden. In accepting complete responsibility for Lennie, George demonstrates the degree of commitment necessary to the Steinbeck hero, and in fact enters the ranks of those heroes. It is ironic that, in this fallen world, George must re-enact the crime of Cain to demonstrate the depth of his commitment. It is a frank acceptance of the way things are.

Slim recognizes the meaning of George's act. When the pursuers discover George just after he has shot Lennie, Steinbeck writes: "Slim came directly to George and sat down beside him, sat very close to him." Steinbeck's forceful prose here, with the key word "directly," and the emphatic repetition in the last phrase place heavy emphasis on Slim's gesture. Steinbeck is stressing the significance of the new relationship between George and Slim. As the novel ends, George is going off with Slim to have a drink, an action Fontenrose mistakenly interprets as evidence "that George had turned to his counter-dream of independence: freedom from Lennie." [Scholar Warren] French suggests that "Slim's final attempt to console George ends the novel on the same compassionate note as that of *The Red Pony*, but Slim can only alleviate, not cure, the situation." Steinbeck, however, seems to be deliberately placing much greater emphasis on the developing friendship between the two men than such interpretations would allow for. Lisca has pointed out the circular structure of the novel—the neat balancing of the opening and closing scenes. Bearing this circularity in mind, it should be noted that this novel about man's loneliness and "apartness" began with two men—George and Lennie—climbing down to the pool from the highway and that the novel ends with two men—George and Slim—climbing back up from the pool to the highway. Had George been left alone and apart from the rest of humanity at the end of the novel, had he suffered the fate of Cain, this would indeed have been the most pessimistic of Steinbeck's works. That George is not alone has tremendous significance. In the fallen world of the valley, where human commitment is the only realizable dream, the fact that in the end as in the beginning two men walk together causes *Of Mice and Men* to end on a strong note of hope—the crucial dream, the dream of man's commitment to man, has not perished with Lennie. The dream will appear again, in fact, in much greater dimension in Steinbeck's next novel, *The Grapes of Wrath*.

The American Dream Is Doomed in *Of Mice and Men*

John H. Timmerman

John H. Timmerman is a professor of English at Calvin College in Michigan and the author of John Steinbeck's Fiction: The Aesthetics of the Road Taken *and* The Dramatic Landscape of Steinbeck's Short Stories.

In the following essay, Timmerman argues that Of Mice and Men *is finely crafted to illustrate the futility of the American dream. The structural framing and foreshadowing within the novella, he asserts, illuminate the work's theme of unfulfilled dreams. For instance, the mountains represent the mystery of death, Timmerman contends, and the death of Candy's crippled dog foreshadows Lennie's similar demise. The development of Lennie's character is also significant. He is more kind and sensitive than other characters in the book; therefore, the fact that he remains a social misfit makes readers question the health of a society that has no place for him. Finally, Timmerman contends that* Of Mice and Men *is memorable because of its themes of friendship and human dreams. Many characters suffer from pangs of loneliness and learn, like Lennie, that there is little to look forward to in their lives.*

Fortunately, few people have been deterred from serious consideration of *Of Mice and Men* by Maxwell Geismar's surprising judgment: "How thin 'Of Mice and Men' is after all, how full of easy sensations it appears upon a little reflection." Lamenting the thinness of the characters—"Lennie . . . seems rather more like a digestional disturbance than a social problem"—Geismar declares that

"Of Mice and Men" is a tribute to Steinbeck's narrative power, to the brilliance with which he clothes such mechanical literary types, to the intensity which somehow gives breath to these poor scarecrows. We see here the dominance of the creative fire over common sense, so that we are held by such apparitions as these characters who, when removed from the framework of the play, crumble under the weight of their own improbability.

Those are a few of his kinder judgments, but regardless of such early reactions, readers have found themselves very much intrigued by Steinbeck's scarecrows. The popular reception of Steinbeck's work had, in fact, grown to the point where he would mutter that fame was "a pain in the ass," partly, of course, because of the demands on time that he would rather give to writing. By the same token, one cannot measure aesthetic excellence by popular reception, but there are excellences in the work itself that account for its enduring appeal.

Steinbeck's Dramatic Art

Shortly after *In Dubious Battle* was published, Steinbeck considered revising that novel into dramatic structure for the stage. After several thwarted attempts at blocking the novel, he gave up the effort. It was probably an impossible task. Although while he was writing *In Dubious Battle*, Steinbeck concentrated on conveying action through dialogue and providing clear character portraits that in novelistic form contain a forceful sense of concentrated action, the novel itself was too unwieldy for successful adaptation to the stage. It is curious that while more films have been made of Steinbeck's work than of the work of any other modern novelist, no film has been made of *In Dubious Battle*—curious because the *movements between* the concentrated actions and the tight sequence of the novel, while difficult for the narrower confines of the stage, lend themselves very nicely to cinematic art. *Of Mice and Men*, however, was written with deliberate staging design;

in fact, over 80 percent of the lines went directly into the play. [Critic] Joseph Fontenrose comments on the artistic technique of the work:

> Each of the six chapters is confined to one scene and opens with a description of the scene; there follows dialogue with entrance and exit of characters. Every descriptive or narrative remark can be considered a stage direction. . . . The chapters can easily be converted, as they stand, into acts or scenes; and this is nearly what was done when *Of Mice and Men* was published and produced as a play in November, 1937. The dialogue was altered very little, and the conversion of description and narrative required more changes in form than in content. As drama or novel *Of Mice and Men* is economical, tightly knit, carefully constructed.

The effect is clear in the novel. *Of Mice and Men* is one of Steinbeck's most compressed and unified works. Nonetheless, it achieves an artistic richness of structure and theme that ranks it among the best of his works. Three items in particular distinguish the novel: the framing and foreshadowing through structure, the development of Lennie's character and the theme of friendship, and the nature of human dreams.

Framing and Foreshadowing

The novel opens with the objective specificity of locale that would mark stage directions, or perhaps cinema. Like a long pan of the camera, the opening scene traces the Salinas River where it "drops in close to the hillside bank and runs deep and green" near Soledad. Following the flow of the river, the scene narrows and becomes more specific in detail, moving from the broad expanse of the "golden foothill slopes" of the Gabilan Mountains to the very small setting of "the sandy bank under the trees," where we find details as minute as "a lizard makes a great skittering" and "the split-wedge tracks of deer." The narrowing vision provides a smooth and gentle transition to the two bindlestiffs [hobos] hunkered by a fire in the evening of the day. The light, too, narrows and focuses, from the broad, golden flanks of the Gabilans to the evening duskiness and the shade "that climbed up the hills toward the top."

The expertly framed opening is precisely echoed and inverted at the close of the novel, where the same two bindlestiffs stand by "the deep green pool of the Salinas River" in the evening of the day. Once again shade pushes the sunlight "up the slopes of the Gabilan Mountains, and the hilltops were rosy in the sun." We find the same, familiarly routine skitterings of birds and animals by the sandy bank, only now a small something has happened. The original title of the novel, "Something That Happened," is precisely the point here; a small thing occurs, however momentous and tragic in the lives of Lennie and George, that goes virtually unnoticed in the ways of the world. Antonia Seixas comments in her article "John Steinbeck and the Non-Teleological Bus" that "the hardest task a writer can set himself is to tell the story of 'something that happened' without explaining 'why'—and make it convincing and moving." Again, as if viewing the scene through a movie camera, we observe the "what" without the explanatory "why." While Lennie stares into the sun-washed mountains, George recreates the dream as he levels the Luger at the base of Lennie's skull.

The mountains that frame the story, as they frame the little thing that happened in the lives of George and Lennie, always carry large significance for Steinbeck. In *The Grapes of Wrath* crossing the mountains represents the entrance into the promised land for the Okies. In *East of Eden*, Steinbeck provides two mountain ranges, one dark and one light, which symbolically frame the struggle between good and evil in the valley between those ranges. In *The Red Pony*, as in *To a God Unknown*, the mountains represent mystery; in 'the former work old Gitano goes to the mountains on Easter to die; in the latter Joseph Wayne witnesses strange, ancient rituals. In

Of Mice and Men also, the darkening mountains represent the mystery of death, carefully sustained in the minor imagery of the heron seizing and eating the little water snakes.

In between the two scenes of the mountains on those two evenings, and in the serene willow grove that, as Peter Lisca points out, symbolizes "a retreat from the world to a primeval innocence," we have the quiet drama of George and Lennie's dream unfolding and unraveling. But this dream is doomed, and Steinbeck provides ample foreshadowing in the novel, most notably in Candy's dog. According to Carlson, Candy's dog has to die because he is a cripple, out of sorts with the normal routine of society, something in the way. With careful detail Carlson describes how he would shoot the dog so that it would not feel any pain: "'The way I'd shoot him, he wouldn't feel nothing. I'd put the gun right there.' He pointed with his toe. 'Right back of the head. He wouldn't even quiver.'" Candy's huge regret is that he didn't do so himself. It would have been kinder to have the dog die by a familiar and loved hand than to have a stranger drag him to his death. The same feeling motivates George as he leads the social cripple Lennie to his dream world. For Steinbeck this act constitutes a rare heroism. Years later he wrote in a letter to Annie Laurie Williams:

> M & M may seem to be unrelieved tragedy, but it is not. A careful reading will show that while the audience knows, against its hopes, that the dream will not come true, the protagonists must, during the play, become convinced that it will come true. Everyone in the world has a dream he knows can't come off but he spends his life hoping it may. This is at once the sadness, the greatness and the triumph of our species. And this belief on stage must go from skepticism to possibility to probability before it is nipped off by whatever the modern word for fate is. And in hopelessness—George is able to rise to greatness—to kill his friend to save him. George is a hero and only heroes are worth writing about.

Dreamers Are Doomed in
Of Mice and Men

Lennie is not the only dreamer in the novel, however, and each of the other dreamers also seems afflicted with the loneliness of nonattainment. Most notable is the woman known only as "Curley's wife," a mere thing possessed by her flamboyant husband. From the start George recognizes the incipient danger posed by Curley's wife, a recognition that proves prophetically true: "'She's gonna make a mess. They's gonna be a bad mess about her. She's a jail bait all set on the trigger.'" But Curley's wife is also caught in a hopeless little valley of small dreams. She dreamed of being an actress, of sweeping Hollywood, but when Curley came along he simply represented escape, and that was better than nothing. When Lennie shares his dream in response to her candor, she exclaims: "'You're nuts. . . . But you're a kinda nice fella. Jus' like a big baby. But a person can see kinda what you mean.'" Similarly, Crooks, the stable hand and another small outcast, has his dream, one of companionship to assuage the terrible, haunting loneliness: "'Books ai'nt no good. A guy needs somebody—to be near him. . . . A guy goes nuts if he ain't got nobody.'" And Candy too, another social outcast, is captivated by the dream: "'Sure they all want it. Everybody wants a little bit of land, not much. Jus' som'thin' that was his. Som'thin' he could live on and there couldn't nobody throw him off of it. I never had none.'"

But through his careful foreshadowing Steinbeck suggests that each dream is doomed. Curley, the flamboyant fighter, stands ever ready to goad someone into a fight, particularly those larger than he, and who is larger on the ranch than Lennie? The dead mouse that Lennie strokes prefigures the dead girl's hair and the impossible dream of rabbits. And George knows these things; he senses the inevitable end. Early in the novel he tells Lennie to remember good hiding places, even as he tells him once more of the dream farm and the "fatta the lan.'"

What keeps these little social outcasts going? What motivates them when all dreams seem doomed? In a sense the large-scale battle of *In Dubious Battle* is played out here in a small, quiet, but equally tragic scene, as if George and Lennie are the Everymen in a microcosmic universe. They are drawn together by the human need born of loneliness. George's words to Lennie, which form a dark refrain in the book, might have occurred equally well in *In Dubious Battle* or *The Grapes of Wrath*: "'Guys like us, that work on ranches, are the loneliest guys in the world. They got no family. They don't belong no place. They come to a ranch an' work up a stake and then they go into town and blow their stake, and the first thing you know they're poundin' their tail on some other ranch. They ain't got nothing to look ahead to.'"

Lennie Is Sensitive and Kind

Even though the dream seems inevitably doomed, that is also at once man's glory—that he can dream and that others participate in the dream. Finally, this sets Lennie apart from the animal that he is imaged as being. At first the novel seems to set forth one more reductionistic pattern of imagery so familiar to Steinbeck's work. Lennie seems little more than an animal in human form: "Behind him walked his opposite, a huge man, shapeless of face, with large, pale eyes, and wide, sloping shoulders; and he walked heavily, dragging his feet a little, the way a bear drags his paws." Lennie bends to the water and drinks "with long gulps, snorting into the water like a horse." After drinking, he "dabbled his big paw in the water and wiggled his fingers so the water arose in little splashes." . . . Lennie [however] rises above the animal in several ways. He is, for example, marked by kindness, a trait that at once sets him above Curley. Lennie is sensitive to the small and the forlorn, and it is no accident that Crooks and Curley's wife confide freely in him. But he does lack the rational acuity to survive in this society; killing Curley's wife is not qualitatively different for Lennie from killing the mouse. As [critic] Howard Levant points out, "The relative meaninglessness of his victims substitutes pathos for tragedy." Clearly, Lennie is not a tragic figure, for he has nothing of the required nobility about him. But in a sense the deeper tragedy lies in his pathos; there is no place for a Lennie in society. Yet in the novel there is a kind of subtle reversal of animal imagery that makes animals of those who establish society's norms that disallow the survival of a Lennie. . . . In *Of Mice and Men*, Curley is closer to the animal in his predatory desire to fight. Oppression of any life is the animalistic trait, the struggle for survival that kills off or hides away the weaker members. For Steinbeck, on the other hand, that human life, which might be observable upon first glance as animalistic, often carries a warm dignity. While Lennie is a social misfit, it may be because society itself is ill.

Although *Of Mice and Men* quickly became one of Steinbeck's most popular works, it met with a great deal of puzzlement. Readers may have expected another angry *In Dubious Battle* from him and got instead this sad little drama of something that happened, something so small it escapes common attention. George walks away at the end just one more bindlestiff. Yet part of Steinbeck's success here lies in investing those small, barely noticeable lives with both pathos and dignity. If, as Carlson points out, there is a right way to kill a cripple, one still wonders why the cripple has to be killed.

But Steinbeck himself was dissatisfied with the novel, largely on aesthetic grounds. With the failed effort to block *In Dubious Battle* for the stage, he wanted very much to succeed with this effort. Steinbeck referred to the book as an experiment "designed to teach me to write for the theatre," and he often spoke of it in perjorative terms such as a "simple little thing," or "the Mice book." Whatever his attitude, the dramatic adaptation, like the novel, was a commercial success, opening at the Music Box Theatre in New York on November 23, 1937, and running for 207 performances.

Steinbeck at this time, however, was back home in California, well into the background work for his greatest achievement, *The Grapes of Wrath*.

Steinbeck Explores the American Dream Through Language, Action, and Symbols in *Of Mice and Men*

Peter Lisca

The late Peter Lisca authored the Wide World of John Steinbeck, *considered the first major study of Steinbeck, which was published in 1958. He also penned* John Steinbeck: Nature and Myth.

In the following article, Lisca contends that Steinbeck's use of symbol, action, and language work together in Of Mice and Men *to suggest a microcosm of all humankind. The symbolic landscape suggests a retreat from the world into a safe place. Here, rabbits become symbols of comfort, representing the American dream in terms that Lennie can understand. Lisca argues that these symbols also set up patterns of action within the work that predict the failure of Lennie's dream. Steinbeck's use of repetitive, ritualistic language complicates this prediction, however, as it suggests that Lennie's dream is not interrupted by his death. Despite these patterns,* Of Mice and Men *is not simplistic. Lisca notes that the characters' free will deepens our reading of these patterns and that the story takes on multiple meanings.*

Concerning [*Of Mice and Men*'s] theme, Steinbeck wrote his agents, "I'm sorry that you do not find the new book as large in subject as it should be. I probably did not make my subjects and my symbols clear. The microcosm is rather difficult to handle and apparently I did not get it over—the earth longings of a Lennie who was not to represent insanity at all but the inarticulate and powerful yearning of all men. Well, if it isn't there it isn't there." To [his friend] Ben Abramson he wrote a similar comment on the book's theme: ". . . it's a study of the dreams and pleasures of everyone in the world."

Such words as "microcosm," "of all men," and "everyone in the world" indicate that the problem he set himself in *Of Mice and Men* was similar to that he had solved in his previous novel, *In Dubious Battle*. But whereas in the earlier work the de-personalized protagonists were easily absorbed into a greater pattern because that pattern was physically present in the novel, in *Of Mice and Men* the protagonists are projected against a very thin background and must suggest or create this larger pattern through their own particularity. To achieve this, Steinbeck makes use of language, action, and symbol as recurring motifs. All three of these motifs are presented in the opening scene, are contrapuntally developed through the story, and come together again at the end.

A Symbolic Landscape

The first symbol in the novel, and the primary one, is the little spot by the river where the story begins and ends. The book opens with a description of this place by the river, and we first see George and Lennie as they enter this place from the highway to an outside world. It is significant that they prefer spending the night here rather than going on to the bunkhouse at the ranch.

Steinbeck's novels and stories often contain groves, willow thickets by a river, and caves which figure prominently in the action. . . . For George and Lennie, as for other Steinbeck heroes, coming to a cave or thicket by the river symbolizes a retreat from the world to a primeval innocence. . . . In the opening scene of *Of Mice and Men* Lennie twice mentions the possibility of hiding out in a cave, and George impresses on him that he must return to this thicket by the river when there is trouble.

While the cave or the river thicket is a "safe place," it is physically impossible to remain there, and this symbol of primeval innocence becomes translated into terms possible in the real world. For George and Lennie it becomes "a little house an' a couple of acres." Out of this translation grows a second symbol, the rabbits, and this symbol serves several purposes. Through synecdoche [a literary device in which a part of something is representative of the whole] it comes to stand for the "safe place" itself, making a much more easily manipulated symbol than the "house an' a couple of acres." Also, through Lennie's love for the rabbits Steinbeck is able not only to dramatize Lennie's desire for the "safe place," but to define the basis of that desire on a very low level of consciousness—the attraction to soft, warm fur, which is for Lennie the most important aspect of their plans.

The Motif of Action

This transference of symbolic value from the farm to the rabbits is important also because it makes possible the motif of action. This is introduced in the first scene by the dead mouse which Lennie is carrying in his pocket (much as Tom carries the turtle in *The Grapes of Wrath*). As George talks about Lennie's attraction to mice, it becomes evident that the symbolic rabbits will come to the same end—crushed by Lennie's simple, blundering strength. Thus Lennie's killing of mice and later his killing of the puppy set up a pattern which the reader expects to be carried out again. George's story about Lennie and the little girl with the red dress, which he tells twice, contributes to this expectancy of pattern, as do the shooting of Candy's dog, the crushing of Curley's hand, and the frequent appearances of Curley's wife. All these incidents are patterns of the action motif and predict the fate of the rabbits and thus the fate of the dream of a "safe place."

Language as Ritual

The third motif, that of language, is also present in the opening scene. Lennie asks George, "Tell me—like you done before," and George's words are obviously in the nature of a ritual. "George's voice became deeper. He repeated his words rhythmically, as though he had said them many times before." The element of ritual is stressed by the fact that even Lennie has heard it often enough to remember its precise language: "*An' live off the fatta the lan'.* . . . An' have *rabbits.* Go on George! Tell about what we're gonna have in the garden and about the rabbits in the cages and about. . . ." This ritual is performed often in the story, whenever Lennie feels insecure. And of course it is while Lennie is caught up in this dream vision that George shoots him, so that on one level the vision is accomplished—the dream never interrupted, the rabbits never crushed.

The highly patterned effect achieved by these incremental [motifs of symbol, action, and language] is the knife edge on which criticism of *Of Mice and Men* divides. For although Steinbeck's success in creating a pattern has been acknowledged, criticism has been divided as to the effect of this achievement. On one side, it is claimed that this strong patterning creates a sense of contrivance and mechanical action, and on the other, that the patterning actually gives a meaningful design to the story, a tone of classic fate. What is obviously needed here is some objective critical tool for determining under what conditions a sense of inevitability (to use a neutral word) should be experienced as mechanical contrivance, and when it should be experienced as catharsis effected by a sense of fate. Such a tool cannot be forged within the limits of this study; but it is possible to examine the particular circumstances of *Of Mice and Men* more closely before passing judgment.

The Power of Free Will

Although the three motifs of symbol, action, and language build up a strong pattern of inevitability, the movement is not unbroken. About midway in the novel (chapters 3 and 4)

Of Mice and Men and the American Dream

there is set up a countermovement which seems to threaten the pattern. Up to this point the dream of "a house an' a couple of acres" seemed impossible of realization. Now it develops that George has an actual farm in mind (ten acres), knows the owners and why they want to sell it: "The ol' people that owns it is flat bust an' the ol' lady needs an operation." He even knows the price—"six hundred dollars." Also, the old workman, Candy, is willing to buy a share in the dream with the three hundred dollars he has saved up. It appears that at the end of the month George and Lennie will have another hundred dollars and that quite possibly they "could swing her for that." In the following chapter this dream and its possibilities are further explored through Lennie's visit with Crooks, the power of the dream manifesting itself in Crooks's conversion from cynicism to optimism. But at the very height of his conversion the mice symbol reappears in the form of Curley's wife, who threatens the dream by bringing with her the harsh realities of the outside world and by arousing Lennie's interest.

The function of Candy's and Crooks's interest and the sudden bringing of the dream within reasonable possibility is to interrupt, momentarily, the pattern of inevitability. But, and this is very important, Steinbeck handles this interruption so that it does not actually reverse the situation. Rather, it insinuates a possibility. Thus, though working against the pattern, this countermovement makes that pattern more credible by creating the necessary ingredient of free will. The story achieves power through a delicate balance of the protagonists' free will and the force of circumstance.

Many Meanings

In addition to imposing a sense of inevitability, this strong patterning of events performs the important function of extending the story's range of meanings. This can best be understood by reference to [Ernest] Hemingway's "fourth dimension," which has been defined by Joseph Warren Beach as an "aesthetic factor" achieved by the protagonists' repeated participation in some traditional "ritual or strategy," and by Malcolm Cowley as "the almost continual performance of rites and ceremonies" suggesting recurrent patterns of human experience. The incremental motifs of symbol, action, and language which inform *Of Mice and Men* have precisely these effects. The simple story of two migrant workers' dream of a safe retreat, a "clean well-lighted place," becomes itself a pattern or archetype which exists on three levels.

There is the obvious story level on a realistic plane, with its shocking climax. There is also the level of social protest, Steinbeck the reformer crying out against the exploitation of migrant workers. The third level is an allegorical one, its interpretation limited only by the ingenuity of the audience. It could be, as Carlos Baker suggests, "an allegory of Mind and Body." Using the same kind of dichotomy, the story could also be about the dumb, clumsy, but strong mass of humanity and its shrewd manipulators. This would make the book a more abstract treatment of the two forces of *In Dubious Battle*—the mob and its leaders. The dichotomy could also be that of the unconscious and the conscious, the id and the ego, or any other forces or qualities which have the same structural relationship to each other that do Lennie and George. It is interesting in this connection that the name Leonard means "strong or brave as a lion," and that the name George means "husbandman."

The title itself, however, relates the whole story to still another level which is implicit in the context of [Robert] Burns's poem.

But, Mousie, thou art no thy lane,

In proving foresight may be vain:

The best laid schemes o' mice an' men

Gang aft a-gley

An' lea'e us nought but grief an' pain

For promis'd joy.

In the poem, Burns extends the mouse's experience to include that of mankind; in *Of Mice and Men,* Steinbeck extends the experience of two migrant workers to the human condition. "This is the way things are," both writers are saying. On this level, perhaps the most important, Steinbeck is dramatizing the non-teleological philosophy which had such a great part in shaping *In Dubious Battle* and which would be fully discussed in *Sea of Cortez.* This level of meaning is indicated by the title originally intended for the book—"Something That Happened." In this light, the ending of the story is, like the ploughman's disrupting of the mouse's nest [in Burns's poem], neither tragic nor brutal, but simply a part of the pattern of events. It is amusing in this regard that a Hollywood director suggested to Steinbeck that someone else kill the girl, so that sympathy could be kept with Lennie.

George and Lennie Need Each Other

In addition to these meanings which grow out of the book's "pattern," there is what might be termed a subplot which defines George's concern with Lennie. It is easily perceived that George, the "husbandman," is necessary to Lennie; but it has not been pointed out that Lennie is just as necessary to George. Without an explanation of this latter relationship, any allegory posited on the pattern created in *Of Mice and Men* must remain incomplete. Repeatedly, George tells Lennie, "God, you're a lot of trouble. I could get along so easy and so nice if I didn't have you on my tail." But this getting along so easy never means getting a farm of his own. With one important exception, George never mentions the dream except for Lennie's benefit. That his own "dream" is quite different from Lennie's is established early in the novel and often repeated: "God a'mighty, if I was alone I could live so easy. I could go get a job an' work, an' no trouble. No mess at all, and when the end of the month come I could take my fifty bucks and go into town and get whatever ever I want. Why, I could stay in a cat house all night. I could eat any place I want, hotel or any-place, and order any damn thing I could think of. An' I could do all that every damn month. Get a gallon whiskey, or set in a pool room and play cards or shoot pool." Lennie has heard this from George so often that in the last scene, when he real-izes that he has "done another bad thing," he asks, "Ain't you gonna give me hell? . . . Like, 'If I didn't have you I'd take my fifty bucks—.'"

Almost every character in the story asks George why he goes around with Lennie—the foreman, Curley, Slim, and Candy. Crooks, the lonely Negro doesn't ask George, but he does speculate about it, and shrewdly—"a guy talkin' to an-other guy and it don't make no difference if he don't hear or understand. The thing is, they're talkin'. . . ." George's explana-tions vary from outright lies to a simple statement of "We travel together." It is only to Slim, the superior workman with "God-like eyes," that he tells a great part of the truth. Among several reasons, such as his feeling of responsibility for Lennie in return for the latter's unfailing loyalty, and their having grown up together, there is revealed another: "He's dumb as hell, but he ain't crazy. An' I ain't so bright neither, or I wouldn't be buckin' barley for my fifty and found. If I was even a little bit smart, I'd have my own little place, an' I'd be bringin' in my own crops, 'stead of doin' all the work and not getting what comes up outa the ground."

This statement, together with George's repeatedly expressed desire to take his fifty bucks to a cat house and his continual playing of solitaire, reveals that to some extent George needs Lennie as a rationalization for his failure. This is one of the reasons why, after the body of Curley's wife is discovered, George refuses Candy's offer of a partnership which would make the dream a reality and says to him, "I'll work my month an' I'll take my fifty bucks an' I'll stay all night in some lousy cat house. Or I'll set in some poolroom 'till ever body goes home. An' then I'll come back an' work another month an' I'll have fifty bucks more." The dream of the farm originates with Lennie and it is only through Lennie, who also makes the dream impossible, that the dream has any meaning, for George. An understanding of this dual relationship will do much to mitigate the frequent charge that Steinbeck's depiction of George's attachment is concocted of pure sentimentality. At the end of the novel, George's going off with Slim to "do the town" is more than an escape from grief. It is an ironic and symbolic twist to his dream.

The "real" meaning of the book is neither in the realistic action nor in the levels of allegory. Nor is it in some middle course. Rather, it is in the pattern which informs the story both on the realistic and the allegorical levels, a pattern which Steinbeck took pains to prevent from becoming either trite or mechanical.

Capitalism Thwarts the American Dream in *Of Mice and Men*

John L. Marsden

John L. Marsden is an assistant professor of English at Indiana University of Pennsylvania.

In the following essay, Marsden examines the role of capitalism in the lives of the characters in Of Mice and Men. *He argues that George and Lennie's dreams of independence and land ownership are thwarted by the powers of capitalism. The migrant workers in the novella, for example, are controlled by the figures in authority who reap the fiscal benefits of their labor. Under their watchful eye, George and Lennie's dreams are viewed as subversive, as the men's personal success is not in the best interest of the capitalist scheme. Ultimately, Marsden contends, capitalist authority triumphs in proving there is no place for Lennie within the system. Although he is an ideal worker in terms of his physical strength, the fact that those in power are unable to control him makes him a liability to be reckoned with.*

In the [1992] film of *Of Mice and Men*, the director, Gary Sinise, departs from Steinbeck's short novel in two important ways: first, the film incorporates panoramic shots of the fertile California countryside and second, there are numerous shots of the "bindlestiffs" working on the land. Without seeking to criticize the film, which is beautifully made, I want to focus on the elements of the novel that these departures throw into relief. Despite the novel's setting, the conquered western frontier never comes into view; similarly, the portrayal of the

John L. Marsden, "California Dreamin': The Significance of 'A Coupla Acres' in Steinbeck's 'Of Mice and Men,'" *Western American Literature*, vol. 29, Winter 1995, pp. 291–98. Copyright © 1995 by The Western Literature Association. Reproduced by permission.

migrant fieldworkers does not extend to a description of the work itself in any detail. Initially, this may seem to be an eva-sion on Steinbeck's part, given the more explicitly political na-ture of much of his previous work. As [critic] Paul McCarthy has pointed out, "*Of Mice and Men* and *In Dubious Battle* dif-fer in that the former lacks widespread violence, class conflict and Marxian ideology." However, while *Of Mice and Men* is marked by the absence of the open spaces of the frontier and the absence of labor, the novel is crucially concerned with both of these things, and with the complex political relation-ship between them.

This relationship between land, labor and capital is ex-plored through the dream of freedom that absorbs first Len-nie, then George, Candy and Crooks. According to [critic] Louis Owens, Steinbeck "saw no cornucopia of democracy in the retreating frontier, but rather a destructive and fatal illu-sion barring Americans from the realization of any profound knowledge of the continent they had crossed." In *Of Mice and Men*, the dream of independence and self-sufficiency appar-ently upheld by the vast spaces of the western frontier does indeed turn out to be "destructive and fatal." What remains unacknowledged, however, in Owens' analysis, is that the clos-ing of the frontier was a direct consequence of the need for a capital-based economy to impose order on and to control the open spaces of the West, and not, as [historian] Frederick Jackson Turner's thesis suggests, simply the result of popula-tion migration. The allocation of virtually all available land to railroad companies and a small number of wealthy farmers through a corrupt system of land grants, the extent of which is amply traced in Carey McWilliams' *Factories in the Fields*, was the most significant factor in exhausting frontier space. The central irony of this development is that while capital "killed" the frontier, it also encouraged the prevailing frontier myth—that of individual freedom—in order to amass a labor force. The dream of independence described in *Of Mice and Men* directly conflicts with capitalist practices, as George, Lennie and the others discover.

Workers Controlled by Authority

The novel opens in what seems to be a fertile wilderness setting in which "the Salinas River drops in close to the hillside bank and runs deep and green," and in which rabbits, raccoons and deer all live among the "golden foothills." However, it is soon apparent that this is not quite virgin landscape: a path has been worn by boys from a nearby ranch and by tramps, while in front of a sycamore limb that has been "worn smooth by men who have sat on it" there is "an ashpile made by many fires." Even the tranquility of the scene is undermined by the fact that it offers only a brief respite on the journey between two jobs. From here we move very quickly to the ranch—at least to the bunk house and the barn—where the bulk of the novel is set. The bunk house both symbolizes and underscores in a very literal way the migrant workers' lack of space and freedom. It is a construction whose apparently simple functional purpose disguises its status as an instrument of control:

> [The bunk house was] a long rectangular building. Inside, the walls were whitewashed and the floor unpainted. In three walls there were small windows, and in the fourth, a solid door with a wooden latch. Against the walls were eight bunks. . . .

This spatial confinement forms more than an ironic contrast to the vast acres outside; it reinforces the economic, social and psychological constrictions on the workers.

[French philosopher] Michael Foucault's *Discipline and Punish* examines the architecture of "discipline," of which both the bunk house and the barn are examples. Since effective control of a large concentrated group is difficult to achieve solely by force (as Curley discovers in his attack on Lennie), observation provides, for Foucault, the key to controlling behavior in a more subtle and successful manner: "the exercise of discipline presupposes a mechanism that coerces by means of observation." The ideal model for such coercion is [political philosopher] Jeremy Bentham's panopticon, in which men are always subject to the gaze of the all-seeing eye of authority. Both the bunk house and Crook's barn are panoptical structures: the "small square windows" of the bunk house, for example, are less suited to their ostensible purpose of lighting the interior than they are to allowing for the observation of what is taking place within. In both buildings, control is established by the authoritarian gaze of the boss and his son Curley. Suspicious of Lennie's silence, the boss punctuates his departure from the bunk house with an arresting glance: "He turned abruptly and went to the door, but before he went out he turned and looked for a long moment at the two men." George is immediately aware of the significance of the glance: "Now he's got his eye on us." A short time later, Candy's description of the boss is disrupted by the entrance of Curley, who immediately fixes the men in his gaze: "He glanced coldly at George and then at Lennie. . . . [H]is glance was at once calculating and pugnacious. Lennie squirmed under the look and shifted his feet nervously. . . . Curley stared levelly at him." On Curley's departure, George turns to Candy for an explanation and, before replying, "the old man looked cautiously at the door to make sure nobody was listening." Almost as soon as he begins to speak Curley's wife appears in the doorway, blocking out the sunlight. Such observation serves to place the characters in what Foucault calls "a state of conscious and permanent visibility that assures the automatic functioning of power."

Foucault's description of the function of observation cannot fully account for the internal divisions among the migrant workers in *Of Mice and Men*, or for the corresponding absence of a collective response. [Sociologist] Peter Blau has sug-

In the Broadway play based on John Steinbeck's novel Of Mice and Men, *actors Broderick Crawford and Wallace Ford portray agricultural workers Lennie and George, respectively. Steinbeck's novel depicts the conflict between the American dream and the realities of a capitalist world.* Peter Stackpole/Time & Life Pictures/Getty Images.

gested that "social values that legitimate opposition to dominant powers, and thereby solidify it, can emerge only in a collectivity whose members share the experience of being exploited and oppressed." While the novel alludes to certain social distinctions—the boss "wore high-heeled boots and spurs to prove he was not a laboring man" and Curley "like his father, . . . wore high-heeled boots"—there is little sign here of the class conflicts which so marked the birth of industrial capitalism in Europe. In fact, the migrant workers in the novel do not [as historian Carey McWilliams writes] "share the experience of being exploited and oppressed" because as the West underwent a period of industrial expansion in which agriculture had become "large-scale, intensified, diversified, mechanized," the notions of individual freedom and individual responsibility fostered by western expansion preempted a collective defense of migrant workers' interests.

George and Lennie's Dream Is Subversive

What distinguishes George and Lennie at the outset from the other more aimless and isolated workers is their shared dream of "a coupla acres." The dream operates as a chorus in the novella, in terms of both its tone and the structure that its repetition defines. It is described on three occasions: first, in the opening scene, as a "pipe dream" that George uses to calm Lennie; then, in the middle of the novel, when it appears that there is a possibility of its realization; finally, near the end, where it functions as a requiem for Lennie. In each case, it is recited in religious tones, as if it were a sacred text: "George's voice became deeper. He repeated his words rhythmically as though he had said them many times before." The reaction that the vision provokes in George himself supports its apparently spiritual or other-worldly qualities: "he looked raptly at the wall. . . . [He] sat entranced with his own picture." This rapture, together with the pastoral vision that it invokes, has led critics such as Owens and [William] Goldhurst to see the dream as an expression of a desire to return to Eden and a pre-lapsarian [before the Fall] world. Owens, for example, suggests that the vision "represents a desire to defy the Curse of Cain and fall of man," while Goldhurst traces a parallel between the migrant workers and Cain, neither of whom "possess or enjoy the fruits of [their] labor."

Because it is so like a litany, however, there is the danger that what the dream actually describes will be overlooked in favor of its allegorical status. In fact, an analysis of its terms of reference suggests that the vision is, more than an invocation of some symbolic Eden, a direct reaction to the physical and psychological conditions imposed by capitalist practices; it is an expression of the desire for self-fulfillment and self-sufficiency. Initially, what is described is sketchy: George tells Lennie that they will "get a coupla acres an' a cow and some pigs. . . . An' when it rains in winter, we'll just say the hell with goin' to work, and we'll build up a fire in the stove and set around it." Later, when the possibility of realizing their hopes seems closer, the description of "a coupla acres" and the comforts they will offer becomes much more detailed, including a "kitchen, orchard, cherries, apples, peaches" as well as a "chicken run" and a "win'mil." This vision is the quintessential "American Dream," a dream founded, of course, on the notion that on the frontier anyone can find success. The dream reveals as much about the nature of power relations in an industrial system as it does about the simple desire for material success. The vision described by George is a reaction to what Foucault calls "biopower," the exercise of which provides for the "subjugation of bodies and control of populations" that a developing capitalist society needs to accomplish: "we'd just live there: We'd belong there. There wouldn't be no more runnin' around the country. . . . No, sir, we'd have our own place where we belonged, and not sleep in no bunk house." The vision unites George and Candy in a reaction to alienation, which is classically the consequence of the separation of labor from the full process of production. Candy's alienation ("I planted crops for damn near ever'body in this state, but they wasn't my crops and when I harvested 'em, it wasn't none of my harvest") would be, for George, resolved by the fulfillment of their shared dream: "when we put in a crop, why, we'd be there to take the crop up. We'd know what'd come of our planting." A corollary is freedom from exploitative working conditions: "It ain't enough land so we'd have to work too hard," George says, "Maybe six, seven hours a day. We wouldn't have to buck no barley eleven hours a day." The "administration of bodies and the calculated management of life," which, for Foucault, is an essential element of capitalism, would be usurped by the realization of the vision of spatial and temporal freedom: "S'pose they was a carnival or a circus come to town, or a ball-game, or any damn thing. . . . We'd just go to her. . . . we wouldn't ask nobody if we could. Jus' say 'We'll go to her,' an' we would."

In discussing their plan, George warns Candy to be careful not to reveal anything because "They li'ble to can us so we can't get no stake." Their plan is potentially subversive because the growing unity between George, Lennie, Candy and even Crooks raises the possibility that they will be able to stake themselves to a few acres of land. This would offer Candy the opportunity to escape the Darwinian consequences of capitalism: "Maybe you'll let me hoe in the garden even after I ain't no good at it." Even the cynical Crooks, who has "seen hunderds of men come by on the road an' in the ranches, with bindles on their backs, an' that same damn thing in their heads," is caught up in the moment: "If you ... guys would want a hand to work for nothing—just for his keep, why I'd come an' lend a hand. I ain't so crippled I can't work like a son-of-a-bitch if I want to." This excitement soon dissipates, however, when he remembers his position, or rather, when he is reminded of it by the one character who is equally isolated and lonely: Curley's wife, who points out that "Nigger, I could get you strung up on a tree so easy it ain't even funny."

The Triumph of Capitalist Authority

Ultimately, however, any system that aims to organize and categorize human life must be confronted by its inherent contradictions, those moments of "power-failure." Foucault points out that "It is not that life has been totally integrated into techniques [of biopower] that govern and administer it; it constantly escapes them." This is particularly true of the American West, where the need for migrant labor conflicts with an important function of authority, which is that it "clears up confusion" and "dissipates compact groupings of individuals wandering about the country in unpredictable ways." The well-documented brutality of the response to any attempt on the part of migrant workers in the West to act collectively may be seen as a consequence of this conflict, for the expression of power is never so unsophisticated as when it is most threatened.

Throughout the novel, Lennie has been portrayed as an ideal worker for the industrial system: he personifies the sheer bulk and strength of labor power. Clearly, though, his actions illustrate that he is beyond the control of authority, and therefore a threat to that authority. This is more than simply dramatic irony; it reveals one of the crucial contradictions inherent in "discipline," the successful expression of which, according to Foucault, "increases the forces of the body (in economic terms of utility) and diminishes these same forces (in political terms of obedience)." Lennie's physical strength is thus a valuable commodity, but because it cannot be controlled it also constitutes a threat to the very system in which it is valued: the same strength that bucks bales of hay kills the wife of the Boss's son. His silence has already been interpreted as subversive both by the boss and by Curley ("By Christ, he's gotta talk when he's spoke to"), and, according to George, he possesses a quality that cannot be tolerated: "He don't know no rules"; in other words, because he can neither be isolated nor coerced, Lennie exists outside the framework of capitalist practices, "beyond the pale." Earlier, George had complained that, without Lennie,

> I could live so easy. I could get a job an' work, an' no trouble. No mess at all, and when the end of the month came I would take my fifty bucks and go into town and get whatever I want. Why I could stay in a cat house all night . . . , get a gallon of whisky, or set in a pool room.

This corresponds exactly with George's vision of the future at the end of the novel but, by the end, it has become a vision of desolation. Lennie's death signifies the end of the dream of "a coupla acres" of land, and George's final recitation of that dream constitutes not only Lennie's last rites, but those of the dream itself. More than simply the "mercy-killing" of a doomed man, it signifies the triumph of capitalist authority.

Curley's Wife in *Of Mice and Men* Struggles Toward Her Own American Dream

Charlotte Cook Hadella

Charlotte Cook Hadella is professor of English and writing at Southern Oregon University in Ashland and the author of Of Mice and Men: A Kinship of Powerlessness.

In the following selection, Hadella argues that although John Steinbeck makes the character of Curley's wife more sympathetic in the stage version of Of Mice and Men, *she primarily remains a misunderstood character. On the surface she serves as an easy symbol—the temptress, Eve, responsible for the downfall of George and Lennie's Eden. Hadella notes, however, that this Eden was doomed before this woman even enters the scene, and she is more like the men themselves than readers at first recognize. Curley's wife has her own American dream, but as she has no true sense of herself as a worthwhile person, her dream remains unattainable. She cannot fulfill her dream, Hadella asserts, because she is not afforded the full humanity of someone who is capable of doing so.*

Since the subject of *Of Mice and Men*, on one level at least, is the destructive power of illusion as it pertains particularly to the American Dream, mythical discourse naturally influences the story. Critics have noted that the Garden of Eden myth "looms large" in *Of Mice and Men*, and Steinbeck appropriates Edenic elements to convey his personal interpretation of the American Dream. The role of woman in the Edenic framework, of course, is that of the temptress, the despoiler of the Garden. That Steinbeck manipulates his story to encompass the mythical interpretation is clear. In a *New York Times* interview in December 1937, while discussing his sources for characters and incidents in *Of Mice and Men*, Steinbeck claimed that he had witnessed Lennie's real-life counterpart's killing of a man, not a woman: "I was a bindle-stiff myself for quite a spell. I worked in the same country that the story is laid in. The characters are composites to a certain extent. Lennie was a real person. He's in an insane asylum in California right now. I worked alongside him for many weeks. He didn't kill a girl. He killed a ranch foreman. Got sore because the boss had fired his pal and stuck a pitchfork right through his stomach. I hate to tell you how many times. I saw him do it. We couldn't stop him until it was too late."

To fit the mythical framework of his story, Steinbeck changes Lennie's victim from a man to a woman. Although George and Lennie's illusion of an Edenic existence would have been shattered just as surely if Lennie had killed Curley, for instance, instead of Curley's wife, Steinbeck makes the woman the instrument of destruction of the land dream. The mythical discourse of the fiction dictates that a woman precipitate the exile from paradise. Consequently, George espouses this concept of womanhood and accepts Candy's assessment of Curley's wife as a "tart" before he ever meets her in person.

Steinbeck, however, counters George's stereotypical condemnation of the woman by undermining the entire scenario of the Garden myth; he intimates that the paradise of the land dream is doomed before Curley's wife ever enters the story. Critics generally agree that the grove in the opening scene, where George and Lennie spend the night before reporting to work at the ranch—the same grove in which George shoots Lennie at the end of the story—symbolizes the dream of owning the farm and "living off the fat of the land." But when Lennie gulps the water from the pool in the grove, George warns him that it might make him sick. "I ain't sure it's good water [George said]. Looks kinds scummy to me." George's comment reveals that, symbolically at least, paradise may already be spoiled. Moreover, later in the play, when George talks about the actual farm that he intends to buy for himself and Lennie, he explains to Candy that he can get the place for a really cheap price, "for six hundred bucks. The ole people that owns it is flat bust." Apparently, the present owners of George's dream farm are not able to live "off the fat of the land," a detail that both he and Candy conveniently overlook. By deliberately bringing this fact to the attention of the audience, Steinbeck creates a tension between George's mythical discourse of the dream life toward which he is striving and the voice of reality, which says that even if George acquired the piece of land that he has in mind, his dream of an Edenic existence would still not be realized.

Curley's Wife Is Misunderstood

Likewise, even as Steinbeck attempts to clarify [Claire] Luce's understanding of the character [of Curley's wife whom] she must portray [in the stage version], his explication is complicated by the same dialogic tension between universality and particularity that exists in the fiction. Finally, abandoning any pretense of specific, concrete description of Curley's wife in his letter, Steinbeck writes: "If you knew her, if you could ever break down the thousand little defenses she had built up, you would find a nice person, an honest person, and you would end up by loving her. But such a thing can never happen." What can and does happen in *Of Mice and Men*, which was originally titled "Something That Happened," is that no one loves Curley's wife. She does not even love herself. Revisions in the story for the play script, however, indicate that Steinbeck was aware of the woman's lack of self-esteem in the novel and attempted to add an assertive dimension to her character in the play. For instance, when she runs into Lennie

Lon Chaney Jr., Betty Field, and Burgess Meredith (from left to right) star in Lewis Milestone's film adaptation of John Steinbeck's novel Of Mice and Men. *Like most of the other characters, Curley's wife (Betty Field) has an impossible dream of her own.* Copyright © Photos 12/Alamy.

in the barn, she has come there to hide her suitcase. She intends to leave Curley as soon as she can sneak away and hitchhike to Hollywood. Instead of merely voicing her dissatisfaction with life on the ranch, she takes specific action; she plans an escape. Even in pursuit of her personal vision, however, the woman has no solid notion of herself as a worthwhile person. Her dream is to be in pictures—to become a cinematic image that occupies no space in the real world. She even imagines that the clothes she would wear in the movies would be the ones she would wear all the time. Thus she will always be just an image, the woman from the silver screen.

Steinbeck's emotional appeal to Luce, "If you knew her . . . you would end up by loving her," underscores the author's frustration with the task of explaining a character out of context whose major function in her fictional text is to be misunderstood, undiscovered as a human being, unknown even to herself. These few lines also reveal Steinbeck's awareness of privileged authorial information that he is unable to impart to his reader. The "you," of course, in Steinbeck's injunction to the actress, is not directed at Luce in particular, but addresses an American society generally in which vulnerable, unfortunate young women must survive. Steinbeck adds, "I hope you won't think I'm preaching," a comment that indicates that he was conscious of, perhaps even embarrassed by, the intense moral tone of his appeal.

The character description in the letter closes with that same peculiar mixture of particularity and universality with which Steinbeck began the sketch: "I've known this girl and I'm just trying to tell you what she is like. She is afraid of everyone in the world. You've known girls like that, haven't you? You can see them in Central Park on a hot night. They travel in groups for protection. They pretend to be wise and hard and voluptuous."

Critical Response to Curley's Wife

Pretend is the operative verb here, and it is upon this question of pretended evil versus innate evil that an assessment of Curley's wife depends. A brief sampling of critical comments from the past three decades suggests that Steinbeck's readers draw various conclusions. Peter Lisca, in his 1958 study, *The Wide World of John Steinbeck*, analyzes recurring motifs of language, action, and symbol in the novel and identifies Curley's wife as a "mice symbol . . . who threatens [George and Lennie's] dream by bringing with her the harsh realities of the outside world and by arousing Lennie's interest." This statement follows Lisca's discussion of inevitability in the novel. To Lennie, the rabbits, and by extension all soft, furry things, represent the dream of owning the farm. But the dead mouse in the first scene of the story signals the inevitable failure of the dream. Lennie destroys soft, furry things—as his killings of mice and of the puppy indicate. Thus, Curley's wife is just another soft, furry thing doomed to destruction by Lennie. Her death is just the "something" that was bound to happen to ensure the shattering of George and Lennie's illusion. Lisca's assessment of the woman is relatively neutral: she brings "the harsh realities of the outside world" to bear upon the events of the story, but she does not necessarily represent evil.

On the other hand, in 1974 both [critics] Mark Spilka and Howard Levant offered scathing interpretations of Curley's wife. According to Spilka, "Steinbeck projects his own hostilities [toward the woman] through George and Lennie. He has himself given this woman no other name but 'Curley's wife,' as if she had no personal identity for him. He has presented her, in the novel, as vain, provocative, vicious . . . and only incidentally lonely." Steinbeck's revision of the woman's role in the play, Spilka wrote, "creates a new imbalance to correct an old one. His sentimentality is the obverse side of his hostility. . . . Only when sexually quiescent—as in death or childhood—can [Curley's wife] win this author's heart." Similarly, Levant observed that the woman "is characterless, nameless, and constantly discontent, so her death inspires none of the sympathy one might feel for a kind or serene woman."

In a 1979 article that analyzes Steinbeck's treatment of women in his plays, Sandra Beatty suggests that Curley's wife "serves to reinforce the theme of loneliness, isolation, and the idea of a personal dream which is central to the play. She commands both our sympathy and respect because of her naive yet genuine pursuit of a life-long dream." Beatty believes that Steinbeck, by not giving the female character a name, "deliberately delineat[ed] her role insofar as it is seen by the male characters in the play." Along this same line, Louis Owens, in *John Steinbeck's Re-Vision of America*, reasons that woman is not the evil in the mythical garden of *Of Mice and Men*. Owens proposes that "the real serpent is loneliness and the barriers between men and women that create and reinforce this loneliness." Thus Steinbeck allows Curley's wife to share in the "yearning all men have for warm, living contact."

Of Mice, Men, and Women

Though all of these critics are analyzing the same character, the differences in the conclusions drawn about her are obvious. These conflicts may be attributed to the levels of discourse in the story that compete for definition, for privileged acceptance by the listener. The fiction does not offer an authoritative or absolute statement on the woman's character. It is not surprising, then, that Claire Luce, wishing to portray the woman in the way that the playwright had conceived of her, had misgivings about her interpretation of Curley's wife. That Steinbeck sincerely tried to satisfy the actress's request for information is apparent, but it is equally clear that his letter could not have helped Luce substantially. By countering his stated conviction that to know this character would be to love her with the forlorn declaration that such a thing could never happen, Steinbeck gives us perhaps the most authoritative statement that he can about Curley's wife. What he reveals in that emotional outburst is that neither the context of the play nor the context of the woman's life allows her full humanity; for this reason, her portrait is incomplete. Nevertheless, even decades after its inception, Steinbeck's little story about something that happened has something to tell its audience, not just of mice and men, but also of *women* who may find themselves in a world where they are unknown and therefore unloved.

Curley's Wife Is Alienated from the American Dream in *Of Mice and Men*

Lesley Broder

Lesley Broder teaches English at Kingsborough Community College in Brooklyn, New York.

In the following article, Broder argues that students can gain a better understanding of Curley's wife if they consider how she copes with loneliness and the loss of her own American dream. Excluded from the male camaraderie of the other characters, she is forced to use her sexuality as both a lure for companionship and a threat against the few people she can dominate. Broder writes that Curley's wife remains alienated throughout the work and no one understands that, like the men in the novel, she too has dreams she has been forced to defer.

O *f Mice and Men* portrays the desperation people experienced during the Depression. The novel is set in rural California, and Steinbeck presents people of different ages, races, abilities, and classes, all of whom are subject to isolation. Although loneliness is inescapable in Soledad, as the name of the town suggests [Spanish for "solitude"], Curley's wife especially suffers because she is the only woman on a ranch where women are treated as nothing more than sexual objects. She therefore develops tactics for surviving loneliness that are markedly different from those used by the men who surround her.

Only Described as Trouble

From the outset, women are categorized loosely as either nurturing or troublesome. Lennie, a mentally retarded individual, has fond memories of his Aunt Clara, who took care of him and entrusted his welfare to George before her death. She is the only maternal representation of women; more often women are cast as conduits to misfortune for men. George and Lennie have been forced to find employment in Soledad because a woman at their former job accused Lennie of rape when he tried to feel her dress. Later, George spends the money he is saving for a ranch on prostitutes. Portrayed only as objects of entertainment and forces of destruction, women repeatedly distract men from their goals.

Curley's wife further adds to this portrayal. Entirely devoid of company, she is the one character who remains nameless. The men acknowledge nothing about her true being, but merely that she is married to the boss's son. She wanders the ranch asking for Curley and using her sexuality to get attention. When Lennie and George first meet Curley's wife, she is described unequivocally in sexual terms.

> She had full, rouged lips and wide-spaced eyes, heavily made up. . . . Her hair hung in little rolled clusters, like sausages. . . . She put her hands behind her back and leaned against the door frame so that her body was thrown forward.

Since her husband pays little attention to her and she has no occupation or friends, to fight desolation she must use her sexual appeal among the ranch hands, whose male camaraderie plainly excludes her.

George puts Curley's wife into the category of "trouble" by warning Lennie that "They's gonna be a bad mess about her. She's a jail bait all set on the trigger." Curley's wife is sensitive to this kind of rejection. When the Black ranch handyman, Crooks, and his white counterpart, Candy, gather with Lennie in the barn, she wants their company and tries to flirt with them. The men respond coolly to her advances and ask that she leave. Discomfited, she responds, "If I catch any one man, and he's alone, I get along fine with him. But just let two of the guys get together an' you won't talk. . . . Think I don't like to talk to somebody ever' once in a while?" Furious and desperate, she attacks each man viciously, but sensing his vulnerability she threatens Crooks in particular: "I could get you strung up on a tree so easy it ain't even funny." Invoking her husband's power when her charms do not work, Curley's wife also draws force from the prevailing racist notion of which laborer she—an utterly powerless white female—could attempt to dominate.

In addition to suffering loneliness as the men do, Curley's wife also lives off dreams as they do. While seducing Lennie, she speaks to him about her unspent potential and a man who wanted to make her a movie star. "Says I was a natural. Soon's he got back to Hollywood he was gonna write to me about it." When this man did not fulfill his promise, she married Curley. In all her dreams, men provide salvation and joy, for happiness is not something she can attain for herself. Ironically and pitiably, the sexuality she uses to cope with her lost dreams results in her death as Lennie pets her hair, then panics and snaps her neck just as Curley's wife confides her cherished fantasies.

Upon her death, Lennie is hunted for destroying Curley's property; thus Curley's wife's death makes George and Lennie's dream of owning land impossible. Predictably, Curley's wife, like the prostitute George visits, serves to lead men astray. As such, Curley's wife is often compared to Eve: unintentionally, her actions bring about the fall of paradise, or in this case, the dream of paradise. While the men mourn the end of their own dream, they have remained oblivious to Curley's wife's fantasies, the dreams she could not easily share with the male companions who so readily dismiss her.

Curley's Wife's Deferred Dreams

By examining the character of Curley's wife, students may consider what happens when women submerge their identity in that of another person. Additionally, *Of Mice and Men* reinforces the idea that women without access to other forms of power often use sexuality to get what they need from men. Students can debate the legitimacy of this: Was Curley's wife to blame for her own death? Did Curley's wife have any other recourse than using her beauty for attention? This subject can lead to a controversial discussion of date rape or the criminalization of prostitution. Those sympathizing with Curley's wife may also see the destructive effects of judging women solely on appearances, and the sometimes dire consequences women face when they flaunt their sexuality. If Steinbeck's novel were paired with Harper Lee's *To Kill a Mockingbird*, students could further discuss how another lonely woman, Mayella Ewell, uses her sexuality for attention and how this affects an entire town in rural Alabama.

Alienation rings through every page of this short novel. Each character faces the loneliness caused by unmet needs and miserable circumstances. Until her conversation with Lennie, Curley's wife is alone in a hostile world. While the men actively work toward realizing their dreams, Curley's wife has no way even to imagine executing her plans, however unrealistic they may be. Her lost dreams become, perhaps, the most poignant dreams of all because she has no one with whom to share them, except in the moments preceding her death. Like her fantasies, Curley's wife herself is cut down without ever having had a chance to develop.

Homelessness Creates Loneliness in *Of Mice and Men*

Winifred Dusenbury Frazer

Winifred Dusenbury Frazer was a professor of English at the University of Florida and the author of The Theme of Loneliness in Modern American Drama.

In the following essay, written about the stage version of the novel Of Mice and Men, *Frazer argues that loneliness in that work occurs as a result of the characters being unable to attain the American dream of owning a home. It is only because of their close friendship that George and Lennie seem more likely than the other laborers to fulfill this dream, but their efforts, of course, are doomed. Frazer says the loneliness of the various characters drives the plot of the work and foreshadows Lennie's death and a life of continuing isolation for the others. This kind of loneliness is tragic, she says, and it is magnified by the homelessness of the characters. Frazer argues that it is only through dreaming of a home of their own that they receive temporary relief from their lonesomeness.*

In one sense Americans are so used to moving that they are never homeless and may speak of a casual hotel room as home, but in another they are forever homeless, because "home" is not the place where they live, but the place where they lived as a child. The popular song of December, 1954, whose subject is "There's no place like home for the holidays," typifies American ways by explaining: "I met a man from Tennessee, and he was heading for Pennsylvania.... From Penn-

Winifred Dusenbury Frazer, "Homelessness," in *The Theme of Loneliness in Modern American Drama*. University of Florida Press, 1960, pp. 38–56. Reproduced by permission.

sylvania folks are headin' for Dixie's Southern shores. . . ." The American is not at home where he lives. His "home town" is his parents' home.

Thomas Wolfe, recognizing that to return to one's former home is impossible, entitled a novel *You Can't Go Home Again*. The American can move forward but not back except in memory. What lonesomeness Americans suffer, with a sentimental attachment to a past home but no hope of regaining it in any practical form. . . .

A treatment of loneliness engendered by homelessness [is evident in] John Steinbeck's *Of Mice and Men*. . . . Set in the Western ranch country of the Salinas Valley, California, mainly on a river bank, in a bunk house and in a hay barn, *Of Mice and Men* is a realistic depiction of the life of transient ranch hands. . . .

The dominant cause of George and Lennie's lonesomeness and of that of all the ranch hands is lack of a home. George and Lennie's dream is: "Someday we're gonna get the jack together and we're gonna have a little house, and a couple of acres and a cow and some pigs and. . . ." The stable buck, Crooks, cynical and doubting, expresses the theme of the play:

> I seen hundreds of men come by on the road. . . . Every damn one of 'em is got a little piece of land in his head. And never a God damn one of 'em gets it. Jus' like heaven. Nobody never gets to heaven, and nobody gets no land. . . . I seen guys nearly crazy with loneliness for land.

Steinbeck has made bitterly real the impulsive hunger of the ranch hand for a home of his own. Nothing of the sentiment of the "little grey home in the West" or "land where the tall corn grows" regulates his dreams. He understands the hard work of a farm; he recognizes that farm animals involve a daily responsibility; but his happiness would be in belonging to the land and to the house and to the animals upon the land. Crooks' opinion proves to be correct, however, that for a ranch worker a farm of his own is as unlikely as heaven. Something in his character makes him forever a hired hand, and never a land owner.

An Unusual Friendship

In this hopeless longing for a home on the land George and Lennie are like the other ranch hands. In their friendship for each other they are not. Steinbeck makes use of their close relationship to point up the loneliness of the typical ranch hand. Their affection—almost a mother-child relationship—is convincingly illustrated by their great pleasure in conversational byplay. To George's "What I could do if I didn't have the burden of you," Lennie usually replies, "I'll go and hide in a cave." George contritely answers, "No, I didn't mean it. Stay with me." Then Lennie leads into the subject dearest to them both. "I will if you'll tell me about the farm." George now has an audience ecstatically rapt in every well-worn phrase. [Author Ralph Waldo] Emerson, for all his words on friendship, has not expressed the feeling so vividly as has Steinbeck in a few short conversations.

That such a relationship is unusual is evidenced in the doubt of the boss that George's interest in Lennie can be unselfish. He suspects that George is taking Lennie's pay. One of the hands, Slim, also is skeptical: "I hardly never seen two guys travel together.... Most hands work a month and then they quit and go on alone." George himself says, "Guys like us that work on ranches is the loneliest guys in the world." "But not us!" continues Lennie, "because ... I got you to look after me ... and you got me to look after you." Steinbeck points up the unusual friendship to enhance the tragedy of George's having to shoot Lennie to save him from being lynched, but also to emphasize the aloneness of the typical ranch hand.

So unusual is the obviously genuine feeling between George and Lennie that their dream of a home seems possible of fulfillment to the old bunkhouse keeper, Candy, and finally

In Carlisle Floyd's opera Of Mice and Men, *based on John Steinbeck's novel, Gordon Hawkins portrays the character of George Milton. The plot of Steinbeck's novel is driven by his characters never achieving their dreams.* AP Images.

even to the cynical Crooks, both of whom beg to be allowed to help in buying a small farm. Crooks goes so far as to offer to work for them for nothing if they will take him along. The friendship blows like a breath of love through the lonely world of the ranch hands, who are moved by it to think all things possible, but it inspires the hate of the cowardly boss's son, and proves in the end an ill-fated relationship among workers destined for loneliness. A kind of meanness, which even the dim-witted Lennie senses, pervades the air of the ranch where the two men start work. George's reiterated warnings to Lennie to stay away from Curley and Curley's wife are well founded, but the inevitability of Lennie's becoming entangled with them makes the warnings fruitless. The sustaining dream of a home, which is so vivid as to inspire other lonesome ranch hands with belief, is blasted at the end by the death-dealing shot from the German Luger.

Loneliness Drives the Plot

In structure Steinbeck's drama resembles the "well-made play" in its careful plotting and its pointing up of properties and incidents which will play an important part in later scenes. Were it not for the fact that the theme of lonesomeness is made so poignantly real, the play would seem melodramatic. It contains several violent climactic scenes, which, if they had not been motivated by the suffering of the characters, would be only sensational. This is not to say that it deteriorates into mediocrity, however, for, instead of imposing the action upon the characters, the violence resulting from their loneliness is a logical outcome of it, and the technique of the plot does not weaken the encompassing theme.

The obvious framework which contains the play is the use of the riverbank scene at the opening curtain and at the closing, with George's admonishing words in the first scene, "Lennie, if you just happen to get in trouble, I want you to come right here and hide in the brush," fulfilled by his shooting of Lennie in the last. In between there are references to the possibility of trouble and to the place by the river, where the two men first camp for the night. After the boss's son speaks to Lennie with a chip on his shoulder, George reminds Lennie, "Look, if you get in any kind of trouble, you remember what I told you to do." The big, stupid man finally remembers, "Hide in the brush until you come for me." Later Lennie, in response to George's warning to stay away from Curley's wife, senses trouble. "Let's go, George. Let's get out of here. It's mean here." Later when attacked by the sullen Curley, he complains to George, "I didn't want no trouble." Finally when he has killed Curley's wife and realizes that trouble has hit him broadside, he rushes to the riverbank, where in darkening twilight like that of the opening scene, George shoots him while describing the "little place," which had been their dream.

Added to the carefully prepared build-up of the likelihood of Lennie's getting into trouble is dramaturgical preparation of the kind of trouble to which Lennie is prone. In the beginning George takes a dead mouse away from Lennie, while Lennie protests that he needs something soft to pet and that he has always tried to be gentle with the mice which his Aunt Clara used to give him, but "I'd pet 'em . . . and then I pinched their heads a little bit and then they was dead." Lennie wishes they could get the "little place" of their own soon, because the soft, furry rabbits would not get killed so easily. To arrive at a ranch where one of the hands is trying to give away a litter of new pups is perhaps what Aristotle would call a possible improbability. It is not long after he has been given a puppy that, as could have been prophesied, Lennie has "petted" it to death. By exposition in the opening scene, George makes clear that Lennie has barely escaped lynching in Weed because of this predilection for fondling soft things.

> You just wanta feel that girl's dress. Just wanta pet it like it was a mouse. . . . You didn't mean for her to yell bloody hell. . . .

And shortly after the men first reach the bunkhouse, Curley's wife, whom George rightly calls "jail bait," appears sluttishly perfumed and evokes the comment from the staring Lennie, "Gosh, she's purty."

As if the forecast by incident and exposition of the kind of trouble coming were not enough, Steinbeck has strengthened the play's structure by the pointed use of Carlson's German Luger. Carlson first produces the gun from the bag under his bunk to shoot Candy's old dog. He cleans it obviously before replacing it. Later when George, having found the dead woman, is seen to rush into the empty bunkhouse, the audience is prepared for Carlson's announcement that his gun is missing and recognizes that it is not Lennie, as the men assume, but George, who has taken it. And while George makes Lennie sit and look across the river in the final scene, it is no surprise to see him slowly draw it from his side pocket.

Thus, it is with [playwright Henrik] Ibsen-like precision that Steinbeck lays the stage, but also with Ibsen-like purpose he portrays the tragic loneliness of life on a Western ranch. The isolation which George and Lennie feel pervades every other character. Candy, the old bunkhouse keeper, who has lost his right hand, clings to his blind, stinking dog, until with despairing resignation, he lets the men shoot the miserable animal because of his recognition that they do it with under-standing pity for his grief and not with brutality. Curley's wife hangs around the bunkhouse relentlessly, although she is not encouraged by any of the men. To the charge that she is a tart, she pleads innocent and claims that she is only lonesome.

> I got nobody to talk to. I got nobody to be with. . . . I want to see somebody. Just see 'em an' talk to 'em.

Crooks, the black stable buck, complains to Lennie:

> You got George. S'pose you din't have nobody. . . . A guy goes nuts if he aint got nobody. . . . I tell you a guy gets too lonely, he gets sick.

Even the boss, after stern questioning of George and Lennie, "relaxes, as though he wanted to talk but felt always the bur-den of his position." After some jocular remarks, which are turned aside by George, who feels that "He's the boss first an' a nice guy afterwards," the boss "realizes there is no contact to establish; grows rigid with his position again."

Loneliness Is Tragic

So besides the loneliness of the ranch hands because of their homelessness, there is in the play the lonesomeness of debili-tated old age, of the Negro because of his color, of the lone woman on the ranch, and of the man in authority. There is a sense of homelessness and temporariness among all these characters and some elemental discussion of the needs of mankind for privacy as well as for companionship. Whereas the hands who live in the bunkhouse long for a room of their own, the black stable buck laments that he must live by himself. George's dream of a farm includes "a room to ourselves," and Candy says to Crooks, as he enters the stable room for the first time, "Must be nice to have a room to yourself this way." But Crooks replies satirically, "All to myself. It's swell. . . . Guys don't come in a colored man's room." There is lonesomeness in being one bunk-inhabitant among many as there is lonesomeness in being segregated. There is lonesomeness in old age and in authority, as there is lonesomeness in being homeless. . . .

Carrying their possessions in blanket rolls, or "bindles," George and Lennie make their first entrance, and in a later scene arrive with them at the ranch bunkhouse, where they stow their few belongings by their bunks. A reminder that all the men are temporarily working at the ranch is Carlson's pulling his bag from under his bunk to take out his gun and the placement of all the hands' possessions from their bags onto the little shelves by their bunks. At the end it is with a "small, cheap suitcase" that Curley's wife arrives in the barn to prepare for her running away from Curley. The suitcases or bindles are used as visual reminders of the homelessness which haunts the characters. They contribute to the theme as well as to the plot.

It is because Steinbeck has made his theme more important than his plot that the play becomes a meaningful aesthetic expression of a phase of American life. The technique of creating suspense by exposition and incident is obvious upon analysis, but its use is justifiable, for the final effect of the tragedy of human loneliness is what remains with the audience. Of far more importance than the plot is the portrayal of the friendship which is blasted; of the isolation of each character; of the mood of meanness which is engendered in the atmosphere of lonesomeness on the ranch; and of the homelessness of the ranch hands. Here loneliness is not only pitiful; it is tragic. . . .

A home remains forever a dream which only temporarily assuages the lonesomeness of the dreamers.

Social Issues
in Literature

CHAPTER 3

Contemporary Perspectives on the American Dream

Reconsidering the American Dream

David Kamp

David Kamp is a contributing editor at Vanity Fair *magazine.*

In the following article, Kamp argues that Americans' concept of the American dream has changed since the term was first coined in the 1930s. Originally, the American dream was thought of as hope for a better, richer, fuller life that was attainable for all who aspired to it. In its current incarnation, however, Americans are focusing on "making it big" or "striking it rich." They take on more and more debt as they strive for bigger homes and the latest material comforts. As a result, Americans are unhappier than ever, Kamp asserts, and they are losing faith in the American dream because its new standards now seem out of reach. Kamp contends that middle-class Americans should be content with the continuity of their current lifestyle, rather than working themselves to death and getting buried under mountains of debt in an effort to live like the upper class.

In recent years, the term [the American Dream] has often been interpreted to mean "making it big" or "striking it rich." (As the cult of Brian De Palma's *Scarface* has grown, so, disturbingly, has the number of people with a literal, celebratory read on its tagline: "He loved the American Dream. With a vengeance.") Even when the phrase isn't being used to describe the accumulation of great wealth, it's frequently deployed to denote extreme success of some kind or other. Last year [2008], I heard commentators say that Barack Obama achieved the American Dream by getting elected president, and that Philadelphia Phillies manager Charlie Manuel achieved the American Dream by leading his team to its first World Series title since 1980.

The Original American Dream

Yet there was never any promise or intimation of extreme success in the book that popularized the term, *The Epic of America*, by James Truslow Adams, published by Little, Brown and Company in 1931. (Yes, "the American Dream" is a surprisingly recent coinage; you'd think that these words would appear in the writings of Thomas Jefferson or Benjamin Franklin, but they don't.) For a book that has made such a lasting contribution to our vocabulary, *The Epic of America* is an offbeat piece of work—a sweeping, essayistic, highly subjective survey of this country's development from Columbus's landfall onward, written by a respected but solemn historian whose prim prose style was mocked as "spinach" by the waggish theater critic Alexander Woollcott.

But it's a smart, thoughtful treatise. Adams's goal wasn't so much to put together a proper history of the U.S. as to determine, by tracing his country's path to prominence, what makes this land so unlike other nations, so uniquely *American*. . . . What Adams came up with was a construct he called "that American dream of a better, richer, and happier life for all our citizens of every rank."

From the get-go, Adams emphasized the egalitarian nature of this dream. It started to take shape, he said, with the Puritans who fled religious persecution in England and settled New England in the 17th century. "[Their] migration was not like so many earlier ones in history, led by warrior lords with followers dependent on them," he wrote, "but was one in which the common man as well as the leader was hoping for greater freedom and happiness for himself and his children."

The Declaration of Independence took this concept even further, for it compelled the well-to-do upper classes to put the common man on an equal footing with them where human rights and self-governance were concerned—a nose-holding concession that Adams captured with exquisite comic passiveness in the sentence, "It had been found necessary to base the [Declaration's] argument at last squarely on the rights of man." Whereas the colonist upper classes were asserting their independence from the British Empire, "the lower classes were thinking not only of that," Adams wrote, "but of their relations to their colonial legislatures and governing class."

America was truly a new world, a place where one could live one's life and pursue one's goals unburdened by older societies' prescribed ideas of class, caste, and social hierarchy. Adams was unreserved in his wonderment over this fact. Breaking from his formal tone, he shifted into first-person mode in *The Epic of America*'s epilogue, noting a French guest's remark that his most striking impression of the United States was "the way that everyone of every sort looks you right in the eye, without a thought of inequality." Adams also told a story of "a foreigner" he used to employ as an assistant, and how he and this foreigner fell into a habit of chitchatting for a bit after their day's work was done. "Such a relationship was the great difference between America and his homeland," Adams wrote. "There, he said, 'I would do my work and might get a pleasant word, but I could never sit and talk like this. There is a difference there between social grades which cannot be got over. I would not talk to you there as man to man, but as my employer.'"

The American Dream as Attainable

Anecdotal as these examples are, they get to the crux of the American Dream as Adams saw it: that life in the United States offered personal liberties and opportunities to a degree unmatched by any other country in history—a circumstance that remains true today, some ill-considered clampdowns in the name of Homeland Security notwithstanding. This invigorating sense of possibility, though it is too often taken for granted, is the great gift of Americanness. Even Adams underestimated it. Not above the prejudices of his time, he certainly never saw Barack Obama's presidency coming. While he correctly anticipated the eventual assimilation of the millions of

Eastern and Southern European immigrants who arrived in the early 20th century to work in America's factories, mines, and sweatshops, he entertained no such hopes for black people. Or, as he rather injudiciously put it, "After a generation or two, [the white-ethnic laborers] can be absorbed, whereas the negro cannot."

It's also worth noting that Adams did not deny that there is a material component to the American Dream. *The Epic of America* offers several variations on Adams's definition of the dream (e.g., "the American dream that life should be made richer and fuller for everyone and opportunity remain open to all"), but the word "richer" appears in all of them, and he wasn't just talking about richness of experience. Yet Adams was careful not to overstate what the dream promises. In one of his final iterations of the "American Dream" trope, he described it as "that dream of a land in which life should be better and richer and fuller for every man, with opportunity for each according to his ability or achievement."

That last part—"according to his ability or achievement"—is the tempering phrase, a shrewd bit of expectations management. A "better and richer life" is promised, but for most people this won't be a *rich person's* life. "Opportunity for each" is promised, but within the bounds of each person's ability; the reality is, some people will realize the American Dream more stupendously and significantly than others. (For example, while President Obama is correct in saying, "Only in America is my story possible," this does not make it true that anyone in America can be the next Obama.) Nevertheless, the American Dream is within reach for all those who aspire to it and are willing to put in the hours; Adams was articulating it as an attainable outcome, not as a pipe dream. . . .

The American Dream on Credit

[The 1960s ushered in] the greatest standard-of-living upgrade that this country had ever experienced: an economic sea change powered by the middle class's newly sophisticated engagement in personal finance via credit cards, mutual funds, and discount brokerage houses—and its willingness to take on debt.

Consumer credit, which had already rocketed upward from $2.6 billion to $45 billion in the postwar period (1945 to 1960), shot up to $105 billion by 1970. "It was as if the entire middle class was betting that tomorrow would be better than today," as the financial writer Joe Nocera put it in his 1994 book, *A Piece of the Action: How the Middle Class Joined the Money Class.* "Thus did Americans begin to spend money they didn't yet have; thus did the unaffordable become affordable. And thus, it must be said, did the economy grow."

Before it spiraled out of control, the "money revolution," to use Nocera's term for this great middle-class financial engagement, really did serve the American Dream. It helped make life "better and richer and fuller" for a broad swath of the populace in ways that our Depression-era forebears could only have imagined.

To be glib about it, the Brady family's way of life was even sweeter than the Nelson family's. *The Brady Bunch*, which debuted in 1969, in *The Adventures of Ozzie and Harriet*'s old Friday-night-at-eight slot on ABC, occupied the same space in the American psyche of the 70s as *Ozzie and Harriet* had in the 50s: as the middle class's American Dream wish-fulfillment fantasy, again in a generically idyllic Southern California setting. But now there were two cars in the driveway. Now there were annual vacations at the Grand Canyon and an improbably caper-filled trip to Hawaii. (The average number of airplane trips per American household, less than one per year in 1954, was almost three per year in 1970.) And the house itself was snazzier—that open-plan living area just inside the Brady home's entryway, with the "floating" staircase leading up to the bedrooms, was a major step forward in fake-nuclear-family living.

By 1970, for the first time, more than half of all U.S. families held at least one credit card. But usage was still relatively conservative: only 22 percent of cardholders carried a balance from one month's bill to the next. Even in the so-called go-go 80s, this figure hovered in the 30s, compared to 56 percent today. But it was in the 80s that the American Dream began to take on hyperbolic connotations, to be conflated with extreme success: wealth, basically. The representative TV families, whether benignly genteel (the Huxtables on *The Cosby Show*) or soap-opera bonkers (the Carringtons on *Dynasty*), were undeniably *rich*. "Who says you can't have it all?" went the jingle in a ubiquitous beer commercial from the era, which only got more alarming as it went on to ask, "Who says you can't have the world without losing your soul?"

The deregulatory atmosphere of the [Ronald] Reagan years—the loosening of strictures on banks and energy companies, the reining in of the Justice Department's antitrust division, the removal of vast tracts of land from the Department of the Interior's protected list—was, in a sense, a calculated regression to the immature, individualistic American Dream of yore; not for nothing did Ronald Reagan (and, later, far less effectively, George W. Bush) go out of his way to cultivate a frontiersman's image, riding horses, chopping wood, and reveling in the act of clearing brush.

To some degree, this outlook succeeded in rallying middle-class Americans to seize control of their individual fates as never before—to "Go for it!," as people in yellow ties and red braces were fond of saying at the time. In one of [political cartoonist] Garry Trudeau's finest moments from the 80s, a *Doonesbury* character was shown watching a political campaign ad in which a woman concluded her pro-Reagan testimonial with the tagline "Ronald Reagan . . . because I'm worth it."

But this latest recalibration saw the American Dream get decoupled from any concept of the common good (the move-

The original concept of the American dream—achieving a fuller and happier life—has transformed into an unattainable need to gain more material comforts and bigger homes, like the mansion pictured, which is in Berclair, Texas. AP Images.

ment to privatize Social Security began to take on momentum) and, more portentously, from the concepts of working hard and managing one's expectations. You only had to walk as far as your mailbox to discover that you'd been "pre-approved" for six new credit cards, and that the credit limits on your existing cards had been raised without your even asking. Never before had money been freer, which is to say, never before had taking on debt become so guiltless and seemingly consequence-free—at both the personal and institutional levels. President Reagan added $1 trillion to the national debt, and in 1986, the United States, formerly the world's biggest creditor nation, became the world's biggest debtor nation. Perhaps debt was the new frontier.

Losing Faith in the American Dream

[A] curious phenomenon took hold in the 1990s and 2000s. Even as the easy credit continued, and even as a sustained bull market cheered investors and papered over the coming mortgage and credit crises that we now face, Americans were losing faith in the American Dream—or whatever it was they believed the American Dream to be. A CNN poll taken in 2006 found that more than half of those surveyed, 54 percent, considered the American Dream unachievable—and CNN noted that the numbers were nearly the same in a 2003 poll it had conducted. Before that, in 1995, a *Business Week*/Harris poll found that two-thirds of those surveyed believed the American Dream had become harder to achieve in the past 10 years, and three-fourths believed that achieving the dream would be harder still in the upcoming 10 years.

To the writer Gregg Easterbrook, who at the beginning of this decade was a visiting fellow in economics at the Brookings Institution, this was all rather puzzling, because, by the definition of any prior American generation, the American Dream had been more fully realized by more people than ever before. While acknowledging that an obscene amount of America's wealth was concentrated in the hands of a small group of ultra-rich, Easterbrook noted that "the bulk of the gains in living standards—the gains that really matter—have occurred below the plateau of wealth."

By nearly every measurable indicator, Easterbrook pointed out in 2003, life for the average American had gotten better than it used to be. Per capita income, adjusted for inflation, had more than doubled since 1960. Almost 70 percent of Americans owned the places they lived in, versus under 20 percent a century earlier. Furthermore, U.S. citizens averaged 12.3 years of education, tops in the world and a length of time in school once reserved solely for the upper class.

Yet when Easterbrook published these figures in a book, the book was called *The Progress Paradox: How Life Gets Better While People Feel Worse.* He was paying attention not only to the polls in which people complained that the American Dream was out of reach, but to academic studies by political scientists and mental-health experts that detected a marked uptick since the midcentury in the number of Americans who considered themselves unhappy.

The American Dream was now almost by definition unattainable, a moving target that eluded people's grasp; nothing was ever enough. It compelled Americans to set unmeetable goals for themselves and then consider themselves failures when these goals, inevitably, went unmet. In examining why people were thinking this way, Easterbrook raised an important point. "For at least a century," he wrote, "Western life has been dominated by a revolution of rising expectations: Each generation expected more than its antecedent. Now most Americans and Europeans already have what they need, in addition to considerable piles of stuff they don't need."

This might explain the existential ennui of the well-off, attractive, solipsistic kids on *Laguna Beach* (2004–6) and *The Hills* (2006–9), the MTV reality soaps that represent the curdling of the whole Southern California wish-fulfillment genre on television. Here were affluent beach-community teens enriching themselves further not even by acting or working in any real sense, but by allowing themselves to be filmed as they sat by campfires maundering on about, like, how much their lives suck.

Wanting It Bigger and Better and Now

In the same locale that begat these programs, Orange County, there emerged a Bill Levitt[1] of McMansions, an Iranian-born entrepreneur named Hadi Makarechian whose company, Capital Pacific Holdings, specializes in building tract-housing developments for multi-millionaires, places with names like Saratoga Cove and Ritz Pointe. In a 2001 profile of Makarechian in *The New Yorker*, David Brooks mentioned that the builder had run into zoning restrictions on his latest development, called Oceanfront, that prevented the "entry statement"—the

---

1. Bill Levitt built low-cost homes in large suburban tracts after World War II, playing a role in making home ownership a key part of the American dream.

walls that mark the entrance to the development—from being any higher than four feet. Noted Brooks drolly, "The people who are buying homes in Oceanfront are miffed about the small entry statement." Nothing was ever enough.

An extreme example, perhaps, but not misrepresentative of the national mind-set. It says a lot about our buying habits and constant need for new, better stuff that Congress and the Federal Communications Commission were utterly comfortable with setting a hard 2009 date for the switchover from analog to digital television broadcasting—pretty much assuming that every American household owns or will soon own a flat-panel digital TV—even though such TVs have been widely available for only *five years*. (As recently as January 2006, just 20 percent of U.S. households owned a digital television, and the average price point for such a television was still above a thousand dollars.)

In hewing to the misbegotten notion that our standard of living must trend inexorably upward, we entered in the late 90s and early 00s into what might be called the Juiceball Era of the American Dream—a time of steroidally outsize purchasing and artificially inflated numbers. As Easterbrook saw it, it was no longer enough for people to keep up with the Joneses; no, now they had to "call and raise the Joneses."

"Bloated houses," he wrote, "arise from a desire to call-and-raise-the-Joneses—surely not from a belief that a seven-thousand-square-foot house that comes right up against the property setback line would be an ideal place in which to dwell." More ominously and to the point: "To call-and-raise-the Joneses, Americans increasingly take on debt."

This personal debt, coupled with mounting institutional debt, is what has got us in the hole we're in now. While it remains a laudable proposition for a young couple to secure a low-interest loan for the purchase of their first home, the more recent practice of running up huge credit-card bills to pay for, well, *whatever*, has come back to haunt us. The amount of outstanding consumer debt in the U.S. has gone up every year since 1958, and up an astonishing 22 percent since 2000 alone. The financial historian and *V.F.* [*Vanity Fair*] contributor Niall Ferguson reckons that the over-leveraging of America has become especially acute in the last 10 years, with the U.S.'s debt burden, as a proportion of the gross domestic product, "in the region of 355 percent," he says. "So, debt is *three and a half times* the output of the economy. That's some kind of historic maximum."

Content with Continuity

James Truslow Adams's words remind us that we're still fortunate to live in a country that offers us such latitude in choosing how we go about our lives and work—even in this crapola economy. Still, we need to challenge some of the middle-class orthodoxies that have brought us to this point—not least the notion, widely promulgated throughout popular culture, that the middle class itself is a soul-suffocating dead end.

The middle class is a good place to be, and, optimally, where most Americans will spend their lives if they work hard and don't over-extend themselves financially. On *American Idol*, Simon Cowell has done a great many youngsters a great service by telling them that they're *not* going to Hollywood and that they should find some other line of work. The American Dream is not fundamentally about stardom or extreme success; in recalibrating our expectations of it, we need to appreciate that it is not an all-or-nothing deal—that it is not, as in hip-hop narratives and in Donald Trump's brain, a stark choice between the penthouse and the streets.

And what about the outmoded proposition that each successive generation in the United States must live better than the one that preceded it? While this idea is still crucial to families struggling in poverty and to immigrants who've arrived here in search of a better life than that they left behind, it's no longer applicable to an American middle class that lives more comfortably than any version that came before it. (Was this not one of the cautionary messages of the most thoughtful movie of 2008, *WALL-E?*) I'm no champion of downward mobility, but the time has come to consider the idea of simple *continuity*: the perpetuation of a contented, sustainable middle-class way of life, where the standard of living remains happily constant from one generation to the next.

This is not a matter of any generation's having to "lower its sights," to use President Obama's words, nor is it a denial that some children of lower- and middle-class parents will, through talent and/or good fortune, strike it rich and bound precipitously into the upper class. Nor is it a moony, nostalgic wish for a return to the scrappy 30s or the suburban 50s, because any sentient person recognizes that there's plenty about the good old days that wasn't so good: the original Social Security program pointedly excluded farmworkers and domestics (i.e., poor rural laborers and minority women), and the original Levittown didn't allow black people in.

But those eras do offer lessons in scale and self-control. The American Dream should require hard work, but it should not require 80-hour workweeks and parents who never see their kids from across the dinner table. The American Dream should entail a first-rate education for every child, but not an education that leaves no extra time for the actual enjoyment of childhood. The American Dream should accommodate the goal of home ownership, but without imposing a lifelong burden of unmeetable debt. Above all, the American Dream should be embraced as the unique sense of possibility that this country gives its citizens—the decent chance . . . to scale the walls and achieve what you wish.

The Dangerous Side of the American Dream

Peter C. Whybrow

Peter C. Whybrow is director of the Semel Institute for Neuroscience and Human Behavior at the University of California at Los Angeles. He is the author of American Mania: When More Is Not Enough.

In the following selection, Whybrow argues that humans are biologically wired for immediate rewards. This circuitry, while once useful for early humans' survival and adaptation, has become overloaded by contemporary man's unconstrained desire for material things. The result is a kind of addictive greed that has made shopping an American pastime. Whybrow argues that the American dream should not be packaged and sold in this manner. Americans, he says, will be better served if they reembrace the prudence and personal responsibility inherent in a less materialistic version of the American dream.

"It's called the American dream," [comedian] George Carlin lamented shortly before his death last year [2008], "because you have to be asleep to believe it." Too bad for the rest of us that Carlin and his signature satire haven't been around for the wake-up call of the current market meltdown. After all, he knew something about the dangers of addiction from firsthand experience. He understood earlier than most that the debt-fueled consumptive frenzy that has gripped the American psyche for the past few decades was a nightmare in the making—a seductive, twisted, and commercially conjured version of the American dream that now threatens our environmental, individual, and civic health.

The United States is the quintessential trading nation. Since the [Ronald] Reagan era, Americans have worshiped the "free" market as an ideology rather than for what it is—a natural product of human social evolution and a set of economic tools with which to construct a just and equitable society. Under the spell of this ideology, and the false promise of instant riches, America's immigrant values of thrift, prudence, and community concern—traditionally the foundation of the American dream—have been hijacked by an all-consuming self-interest.

The astonishing appetite of the American consumer now determines some 70 percent of all economic activity in the United States. And yet in this land of opportunity and material comfort—where we enjoy the 12-inch dinner plate, the 32-ounce soda, and the 64-inch TV screen—more and more citizens feel time-starved, overworked, and burdened by debt. Epidemic rates of obesity, anxiety, depression, and family dysfunction are accepted as the norm.

It is the paradox of modernity that as choice and material prosperity increase, health and personal satisfaction decline. That is now an accepted truth. And yet it is the rare American who manages to step off the hedonic treadmill long enough to savor his or her good fortune. Indeed, for most of us, regardless of what we have, we want more, and we want it now. The roots of this conundrum—of this addictive striving—are found in our evolutionary history. As creatures of the natural world, having evolved under conditions of danger and scarcity, we are by instinct reward-seeking animals that discount the future in favor of the immediate present. As a species, we are biologically ill-suited to handle the seductive prosperity and material riches of contemporary America. A novel experience, it is both compelling and confusing.

Wired for Immediate Rewards

Brain systems of immediate reward were a vital survival adaptation millennia ago when finding a fruit tree was a rare delight, and dinner had a habit of running away or flying out of reach. But living now in relative abundance, when the whole world is a shopping mall and our appetites are no longer constrained by limited resources, our craving for reward—be that for money, the fat and sugar of fast food, or the novel gadgetry of modern technology—has become a liability, a hunger that has no bounds. Our nature has no built-in braking system. More is never enough.

That the human animal is a curiosity-driven pleasure seeker easily seduced is of no surprise to the behavioral neuroscientist. It is clearly established that overloading the brain's ancient reward circuits with excessive stimulation—through drugs, novel experience, or unlimited choice—will trigger craving and insatiable desire. Brain anatomy helps us understand why this is so.

The human brain is a hybrid: an evolved hierarchy of three brains in one. A primitive "lizard" brain, designed millennia ago for survival, lies at its core and cradles the roots of the ancient dopamine reward pathways. When the dinosaurs still roamed, around this reptilian pith there evolved the limbic cortex—the deepest cortical lobe—of the early mammalian brain, which is the root of kinship behavior and nurturance. The evolution of mammals is marked by a continuous expansion of this cortex, with the prefrontal lobes of the human brain—the powerful information-processing or "executive" brain that distinguishes Homo sapiens within the primate lineage—emerging only recently, within the last two hundred thousand years.

With the three brains working in harmony, the human animal has extraordinary adaptive advantage, as is evident from the success we have achieved as a species. Through a process of continuous learning—orchestrated by the executive brain—the risks and rewards inherent in changing circumstance are carefully assessed and the personal and social consequence of what we do is remembered to future benefit. But there is a catch. Despite our superior intelligence, as in all animals, we remain driven by our ancient desires. Desire is as vital as breathing. Indeed, in human experience, when desire is lost we call it anhedonia—or depression—and consider it an illness. But, as George Carlin understood, when the brain's reward circuits are overloaded or unconstrained, desire can turn to craving and an addictive greed that subverts executive analysis and common sense.

The Material Dream

Desire fuels the vital engines of commerce: self-interest, novelty seeking, and social ambition. It was Adam Smith—the 18th-century Scottish philosopher and capitalism's patron saint—who first argued the value of harnessing what he called "self love" (instinctual self-interest) within the give and take of a market framework to create a self-regulating economic order. Although he recognized that the human creature left unchecked has a propensity for greed, Smith maintained that in a free society overweening self-interest is constrained by the wish to be loved by others (the limbic brain's drive for attachment) and by the "social sentiment" (empathic and common-sense behavior) that is learned by living in community. Therefore, with the adoption of a few rules—such as honesty in competition, respect for private property, and the ability to exchange goods for money—personal desire can be safely liberated to prime the engines of economic growth. Self-love will be simultaneously molded to the common good by the complex personal relationships and social order in which the "free" market operates; self-interest will ultimately serve the common interest. Experience tells us that locally capitalized neighborhood markets, founded on an interlocking system of self-interested exchange, do in fact sustain their own rational order.

But Smith lived before the invention of the megacorporation, instant global communication, the double cheeseburger,

Shoppers crossing the street at the Grove Shopping Center in California. Peter C. Whybrow argues that today's materialistic version of the American dream is addictive and unsustainable. AP Images.

and hedge funds. Today the tethers that once bound self-interest and social concern into closely knit economic communities, and which gave us Smith's enduring metaphor of an "invisible hand" balancing market behavior, have been weakened by an intrusive mercantilism that never sleeps.

Since the 1950s, rapidly advancing technologies have removed the physical limitations once placed upon human activity by darkness and distance, thus diminishing the natural barriers to free-market exchange. The United States, as a great trading nation, applauded these advances and sought to drive economic growth further by limiting government regulation of markets, as prescribed by the economist Milton Friedman and the Chicago school. Beginning in the late 1980s, as the Soviet Union crumbled and the Internet was commercialized, Smith's engines of economic growth—self-interest, curiosity, and social ambition—were supercharged with the conviction that Homo economicus, a presumed rational being, was capable of self-policing. Freed of constraint, markets would magically regulate themselves, delivering to the American people an ever-increasing prosperity. Believing we had perfected the consumer-driven society, credit laws were relaxed and borrowing encouraged. The American dream was no longer a promise based upon old notions of toil and patience: It was immediate and material.

The idea was simple and irresistible. It tapped deep into the nation's mythology, and for a brief moment during the exuberant years of the dot-com bubble in the 1990s, the American dream was made material. Horatio Alger's story was once again our story—the American story—but this time on steroids. Temptation was everywhere. And true to our instinctual origins, we were soon focused on immediate gratification, ignoring future consequences. Shopping became the national pastime, and at all levels of society we hungered for more— more money, more power, more food, more stuff.

Dreams Should Not Be Packaged and Sold

This incarnation of the American dream was dangerously addictive, and unsustainable. America's productivity per person, per hour is comparable to that of most European nations, but our material consumption per capita is greater by one-third. We finance the difference by working longer hours, sleeping less, cutting back on vacations, neglecting our families, and taking on huge amounts of debt. Before 1985, American consumers saved on average about 9 percent of their disposable income, but by 2005 the comparable savings rate was zero as mortgage, credit-card, and other consumer debt rose to 127 percent of disposable income. With Uncle Sam similarly awash in red ink, America had transformed itself from the world's bank to a debtor nation. Adam Smith's invisible hand had lost its grip.

The financial meltdown, which began as the subprime-mortgage crisis, has finally brought home the inherent dangers of our reward-driven, shortsighted behavior. As the housing bubble inflated, both Wall Street financiers and ordinary Americans began to believe that real-estate values would never fall. With prices of homes skyrocketing 15 percent to 20 percent each year, the family home was mistaken for a piggy bank—another asset to borrow against when struggling to finance an overstretched lifestyle. With no down payment, adjustable interest rates, and deregulated borrowing practices, the challenge became, as the historian George Dyson puckishly asked, "Can you have your house and spend it too?"

The worst, we now know, was still to come. As part of the scramble toward "freeing" the market, America's big investment banks had become exempt from Depression-era regulations that specified the capital reserves they were required to hold against losses. Instinctual desire, abetted by its wily cousin speculation, became greed. Avarice was rampant. The analytical powers of the executive brain were placed in thrall to the lizard. Clever people were now manipulating the money markets without future concern. Mortgage-backed securities, credit derivatives, default obligations, and other mysterious financial instruments designed to limit risk were packaged and repackaged to create unknown trillions of imaginary wealth. Homo economicus had been too clever by half. In reality, when the meltdown began, few people—even the financial gurus—truly understood what was happening. Caught in a web of our own creation, we had fooled ourselves about the risks involved, and then the instruments we created fooled us. With the nation's financial system at the brink of disaster we found ourselves rudely awake.

The conflict between fame, fortune, and the corrupting power of money is a perennial source of fascination in America. *Road Show*, the much-repackaged story by Stephen Sondheim and John Weidman of the Mizner brothers and their get-rich-quick schemes, recently played in New York. The characters of Addison, the flapper-age dreamer who helped define the architectural vision of [the posh Florida retirement communities of] Palm Beach and Boca Raton in the 1920s, and Wilson, his manipulative huckster brother, together embody the striving that many Americans find irresistible—the urge to act out the American dream in material representation.

But dreams are more than material. Dreams cannot be packaged and placed on sale in the shopping mall. The American dream is not found in a house that one cannot afford, a new refrigerator, or a 64-inch TV, for as reward-driven creatures we quickly grow tired of such novelties. No, dreaming is a state of mind that binds the brain in harmony. For each of us our dreams are an evolving work of the imagination, built upon an elusive inner reality that is shaped by emotion and experience—an intuitive sense of future possibility that binds instinct and hope with common-sense analysis.

Achieving the Good Life

As a guiding metaphor, the American dream holds a unique place in American culture and it will continue to do so. While the American Constitution, grounded in the Enlightenment, draws upon a faith in human reason, to dream is part of the émigré package, which is integral to our never-ending search for El Dorado. Americans are a migrant people defined by movement and change. By temperament we tend toward restlessness, optimism, curiosity, risk taking, and entrepreneurship—just as Alexis de Tocqueville described in *Democracy in America*. The same qualities of mind kindled the novus ordo seclorum—the "new order of the ages"—that was the dream of the Founding Fathers and is proclaimed still on the back of each U.S. dollar bill.

Somewhere along the road to affluence, caught up in the excitement of global markets, a virtual world of electronic wizardry, and immediate material reward, American culture has lost sight of the prudence and personal responsibility that are essential to realizing our founding hopes and dreams. What is the purpose of the journey in this land of opportunity when individual social mobility lags behind that of Europe, when 45 million souls are without health insurance, and when our educational system is badly broken? Now, with reality challenging the laissez-faire ideology of recent decades, we have the opportunity to take stock with a renewed self-awareness, curb our addictive striving, and reach beyond immediate reward to craft a vigorous, equitable, and sustainable market society—one where technology and profit serve as instruments in achieving the good life and are not confused with the good life itself.

The dream that material markets will ultimately deliver social perfection and human happiness is an illusion. Perfection does not exist in nature. Nature is infinitely more pragmatic. In nature it's all a matter of dynamic fit—of living creatures striving for balance with their surroundings. To paraphrase the novelist Anaïs Nin, the dream is always running ahead: "To catch up with it, to live for a moment in unison with it, that is the miracle." George Carlin would have agreed.

The American Dream Is Becoming Harder to Achieve for Immigrants

Judy Keen

Judy Keen is a contributing editor for the national newspaper USA Today.

In the following article, Keen argues that the American dream is becoming more elusive for America's immigrant small business owners. Many are using their life savings to keep their restaurants, dry cleaners, and neighborhood shops afloat. After laying off employees and working long hours, some of these businesses are hoping to survive the current economic recession. Others have simply closed their doors. As Keen notes, while big businesses receive government bailouts, small-business owners' pleas to President Obama for support have gone unanswered.

Raudel Sanchez's American dream was so strong that he tied a few possessions around his waist in 1967 and swam across the Rio Grande into Texas.

"I wanted to make a better life in America," says Sanchez, 63. "My dream was bringing my family here and working together."

Sanchez, now a U.S. citizen, joined a brother in Chicago after crossing the border near Laredo, Texas. He worked as a butcher, making $1.85 an hour, and took a second job at a candy factory. He often worked 14 hours a day. He saved his earnings and eventually brought his wife, siblings and parents—who are now in their 90s—to Chicago.

Eventually, he opened several small businesses and built a comfortable life for himself and his family. But now, the recession has hit him hard. He has sold one of his three clothing stores and a restaurant, resulting in layoffs of several immigrant workers. He's considering selling a second store.

Sanchez's story reflects how immigrant-owned businesses—a key part of the U.S. economy—are being threatened by the recession. About 1.5 million immigrants own U.S. businesses, according to a study for the Small Business Administration by Rob Fairlie, an economics professor at the University of California–Santa Cruz. He found that immigrants are 30% more likely to start a business than non-immigrants. They account for 11.6% of all U.S. business income.

Immigrant-Owned Businesses Hurting

Many immigrants started with nothing and built businesses that support them and their extended families and communities.

They epitomize the American dream: Work hard and you can build a good life.

With customers spending less and banks less willing to loan money, some immigrant entrepreneurs are wondering whether that's still true.

A few years after arriving here, Sanchez bought a foreclosed house, then three more. He sold two of them in 1985 and used the money to open Sanchez Bros. Western Wear, a clothing store. He expanded to two more stores in the suburbs, bought a restaurant and started a record label for Mexican music.

He tried to run his businesses cautiously: He paid cash for merchandise and didn't use his line of credit at the bank. When people stopped buying $1,000 cowboy boots, he stocked $400 pairs.

Now they aren't selling, even on sale. "Every year we've seen a decline" in sales, he says.

Besides selling two of his businesses, Sanchez has stopped advertising. He laid off most employees, and now family members are behind the counters.

The record label is down to its last two acts. "I had a meeting with my family and told them we've got to work more and more hard," he says.

Sanchez believes his seven children and nine grandchildren will build successful lives here. He's sure the economy will rebound.

"Maybe next year," he says. Still, he's wondering about his future at a time when he should be planning retirement.

"I still believe in this dream I had many years ago," he says. "The only thing is, you have to work hard."

When Hard Work Is Not Enough

Niall Freyne's dream was snatched away by the recession.

Freyne, an Irish immigrant, closed Galway Tribes Irish Pub last month [May 2009] after lunch and weeknight business dwindled along with his customers' confidence in the economy.

"We just couldn't hang on," says Freyne, 43, who opened the restaurant in 2005 in suburban Frankfort, Ill. "We've already lost so much: all of our life savings, all of the equity in our home."

Freyne wrote a letter to President [Barack] Obama asking why small businesses like his can't get a federal bailout—he says he got no reply—and he held out hope until the last minute that some generous millionaire would rescue him. That didn't happen either, and now Freyne isn't sure how he'll support his wife, Dorothy, and son James, who is 6, or what will become of his 42 employees.

"I feel like I've let everybody down," he says. "I can't control the economy, and that's what killed me."

Diners at Taqueria El Meson in Cicero, Illinois, owned by Jose Torres, who is originally from Mexico. The current economic recession has hurt many immigrant businesses, putting the American dream further out of reach. AP Images.

Fighters but Vulnerable

People who leave their countries to pursue success in the USA often are risk-takers who are optimistic and willing to work especially hard to build successful futures for their children and grandchildren, says Allert Brown-Gort, associate director of the Institute for Latino Studies at the University of Notre Dame.

In difficult economic times, "immigrants are much more likely to battle it out for longer," he says, in part because they realize that "success or failure is really on them, and this is going to have an effect for generations to come."

Because immigrant business owners—particularly those who operate stores or restaurants—often depend on their own communities, they can be "more vulnerable in these downturns," says Gregory DeFreitas, an economist at Hofstra University. For the same reason, recovery will come more slowly to immigrant businesses, he says.

Striving for the American Dream

Susan Patel inherited her American dream from her father, Tulsi, and uncle Mafat, immigrants from India who founded Patel Brothers, a national chain of 41 Indian grocery stores.

Last year [2008], Susan Patel bought Patel Brothers Handicrafts & Utensils, a small Chicago shop that sells kitchen items and Hindu statues and temples, from her father. Since then, she has watched several of the Indian and Pakistani businesses that line Devon Avenue close and stopped paying herself a salary to avoid laying off her two employees.

"We've all had to adjust," says Patel, 33, but she's confident she can survive the recession. She feels obliged to keep her store open to help the neighborhood get through the recession. "If I close, customers may not come to this area at all," she says.

Patel's uncle came here from Bhandu, a rural Indian village, in the late 1960s. Her parents, Tulsi and Aruna, followed in 1971. Everyone shared a house, and Patel's parents worked in factories.

"They saved their money so they could have the American dream," she says. In 1974, they bought a small grocery. More relatives emigrated from India to join the growing throng in the Patel home, Patel says, and more stores and a line of Indian food followed. The family bought restaurants, travel agencies and real-estate companies, and the two brothers' children work in them.

Patel believes immigrant-owned businesses are more likely to make it through the recession because owners often invest their life savings—and their lives—in them. "Everyone works all the time," she says. "At the dinner table, all we talked about was business. It's all we knew."

Patel's goals are identical to those that led her parents to risk everything and come here: "just to make it, to be a success."

Confident in the Economy

It will take more than a recession to threaten the dreams of many immigrant business owners who left their homelands because of political turmoil.

Christos Koskiniotis, 46, and his mother, Panayiota Koskiniotis, 67, own Four Seasons Cleaners. They came here in the 1970s from Greece after government coups forced his late father to close the cafes he owned.

The dry-cleaning business is stable for now, Christos Koskiniotis says. His mom is unfazed because she has "seen everything in her life," he says.

Their confidence in their plan for a better life in the USA is unwavering. "For the long term, this is the best place to be," he says. "You're going to hit rough spots no matter where you're at. . . . I don't think the American dream is ever going to die. To think that would be like giving up on hope."

Dana Kapacinskas, 48, moved here from Kounas, Lithuania, in 1979, during the country's occupation by the Soviet Union. The dream that propelled her family was simple: "Freedom. At that time in the Soviet Union, you couldn't move, you couldn't go anywhere. They would follow you," she says.

The family started a bakery/deli here that grew over time. Racine Bakery now has more than 25 employees and distributes its baked goods to area supermarkets. Business hasn't been affected much by the recession, Kapacinskas says, "maybe because it's comfort food. . . . People still have to eat."

Things are going well enough that the bakery donates food to area churches, schools and non-profit groups. Kapacinskas says she, her parents and brother were motivated to improve their lives and demonstrate to people in their new country that they were willing to work hard.

"I was very eager and I had a good work ethic and I saw the opportunities," she says. "We left our friends and missed our family, but the freedom and the opportunities were unlimited."

That's what Freyne thought, too. He opened Galway Tribes after working at hotels and restaurants in Ireland and the USA. He bought the land and built the place, furnishing it with items imported from Ireland.

"We were making it. We were fine, and then about a year ago the economy started going down a bit and people stopped coming out during the week," Freyne says. Then a new assessment a few months ago pushed his property taxes beyond what he could afford. "We just couldn't survive on weekends alone," he says.

Freyne wants to believe that his American dream can somehow be revived when the economy improves.

"You can't know when that will happen," he says. "I put my blood, sweat and tears in this place. It's a sad story."

The American Dream Is Alive and Well

Stephen Moore

Stephen Moore is The Wall Street Journal *editorial board's senior economics writer.*

In the following essay, Moore expresses his views on some pressing questions about the American economy. He acknowledges that economic fairness seems to have declined in America, as the wealthiest people are earning an increasing share of America's income. These gains, however, have not necessarily come at the expense of America's poor. The latter, Moore says, have made their own significant advances. The middle class is also doing better today, with families earning more than they did thirty years ago. While Moore agrees that athletes, entertainers, and professionals will continue to earn extremely high salaries, he does note that women and African Americans have experienced the fastest income gains since the 1980s, suggesting a decline in discrimination against these groups. Finally, Moore argues that taxing the rich is not the best way to redistribute wealth.

With the U.S. economy in a fragile state, politicians are again debating the age-old question: Should America's economic policies be geared to increasing the rate of economic growth or to promoting economic fairness through income redistribution? During this election year [2008], some have argued that the last quarter-century has given rise to a new "gilded age" in which the privileged have done supremely well but the lower income earners have made no progress. A different view sees an upwardly mobile society in which those who get ahead fastest do so through their hard work, risk-taking, and grit. Let's find out what's actually happened.

Stephen Moore, "Upwardly Mobile America?" *The American*, vol. 32, September-October 2008, pp. 32–35. Copyright © 2008 American Enterprise Institute for Public Policy Research. Reproduced with permission of The American Enterprise, a national magazine of Politics, Business, and Culture (TAEmag.com).

Has the gap between the rich and the poor been getting larger?

The answer to this question is that it depends on how you measure things. If we concentrate on the share of wealth that is earned by the richest 1, 5, or 10 percent, then yes, over time, the rich have corralled a larger share of the wealth. For example, in 1980 the wealthiest 1 percent and 5 percent of Americans earned 8 percent and 19 percent of the nation's total income respectively. But by 2006 those percentages had jumped to 22 percent and 36 percent. The richest Americans now earn a larger share of income than at any time since the Roaring '20s. It is also true that over the past quarter-century the share of income that has gone to the lowest income group (the bottom 20 percent) has fallen from 15 percent to 12 percent. So on this basis it would appear that "economic fairness" has declined in America.

Have the income gains by the rich come at the expense of the middle class and the poor?

Since 1983, every income group has seen an advance in after-tax income. Yes, the gains of the very rich have increased the fastest. But that is in part because of a statistical illusion. When poor people earn more over time, they move into the middle class or the upper class and are no longer classified as poor. Consider someone who was earning $20,000 a year and saw her income move to, say, $50,000 as she moved up the career ladder. That 150 percent gain in income isn't apparent, because we no longer categorize her as poor. But every penny of income gain by a rich person is counted, because there is no higher income class she can move into.

Another problem with comparing the distribution of income from one point in time with another is that up to 1.5 million new immigrants enter the United States every year. A fairly high percentage of these immigrants start at the bottom of the income ladder, replenishing the people who are at the bottom rungs. This creates the impression that poor people do not make significant progress in the American labor force.

Is there really a 'war against the middle class' in America as claimed by people such as CNN's Lou Dobbs?

Well, if the middle class is fighting a war, they've been winning.... In 1967 the average middle-class pre-tax income was about $40,000; in 2005 it was about $60,000. And this does not include the increased generosity of non-wage and non-salary benefits such as healthcare, pensions, flexible work-weeks, and more family leave, vacation, and holidays.

Most economists agree that when these income numbers are adjusted by a more accurate inflation measure—one that takes full account of the improved quality of the products we now have access to, such as cell phones, laptop computers, and new medical technologies, for example—the purchasing power of the American middle-class family is about one-third higher today than in the 1970s.

The Census Bureau family income data indicate that in 1967 one in 20 families had an income of $100,000 or more (in today's dollars). In 2005 one in six families did. There are three times as many families earning more than $75,000 a year today than there were in 1967.

Is there much income mobility in America?

Yes. Income mobility studies track what happens to the economic fortunes of real people and families over time. It turns out the middle class and the poor have experienced much bigger gains over the last several decades than originally thought. What's more, their gains have been even larger than those of the rich.

A 2007 study by the Treasury Department tapped into IRS [Internal Revenue Service] data to observe family incomes over two periods, 1987 to 1996 and 1996 to 2005. During both periods, the poorer a household was at the start, the more rapid that family's subsequent income gain. Average income for the poorest households more than doubled from 1996 to 2005. Perhaps even more stunning is that all income groups gained over the period, except for the super-rich, or the top 1 percent. That's because people who make a very high income in a few years don't always maintain that high income. Think of the many stories of NFL football stars who make millions of dollars before the age of 30 but then retire after an injury and see their earnings go way down.

The Federal Reserve Bank of Dallas looked at the same income mobility data over the time period 1975 to 1991. It found that 95 percent of poor households in 1975 were not poor by 1991. Three out of four of the "near poor" (the bottom 20 to 40 percent in family income) climbed into the middle class or higher over this period.

Does age have much to do with income status?

Yes. For example, an analysis by the Minneapolis Federal Reserve found that the average age of the heads of households in the bottom quintile is 66. A lot of people who are labeled as "poor" are senior citizens, who are retired and have little income but many assets.

How likely are people to break out of poverty from one generation to the next?

A recent study on income mobility, funded by the Pew Charitable Trusts, compares the economic status of parents in the late 1960s and early 1970s with the income level of their children in recent years. The study confirms that kids from wealthy families have a head start in life, but not an insurmountable lead. Of those children who grow up in poor households, more than half are not poor as adults.

The latest *Forbes* list of the 400 richest people confirms that America remains an opportunity society and that it's not easy to stay perched atop the wealth ladder for long. While some are on the list due to dynastic wealth, 270 of the 400—almost 70 percent—amassed fortunes by giving the rest of us products we want.

Don't the rich engage in conspicuous consumption and spend much more than the middle class and poor?

Some people who are fabulously rich do buy Ferraris and yachts and dine on lobster and champagne every night. But they are the exceptions. Overall consumption is the great equalizer in America. Sam Walton, the founder of Wal-Mart, was one of the richest men in history and he drove around in a pickup truck most of his life. According to calculations by former Labor Department economist Diana Furchtgott-Roth, who has analyzed Bureau of Labor Statistics data on household spending patterns, the wealthiest fifth of Americans now consume $28,272 a year per person compared to $15,843 for the middle class and $11,247 for the poor. It's a sign of the growing affluence of the poor that the single largest increase in expenditures for low-income households over the past 20 years was for audio and visual entertainment systems, which were up 119 percent.

Are there other ways that the income data distort our perception of the gap between rich and poor?

Yes. One reason that high income families have higher earnings than low income families is that high income families have more workers. For example, the average household in the lowest income quintile has only, on average, about half a person working (meaning many of the households in that quintile have no one working at all). But the average high income family has two people working, usually a husband and a wife. It is also true that many forms of income that flow to the poor, such as government benefits, are not included in official calculations. When all sources of income are included, households in the lowest 20 percent of the income scale saw a 12 percent rise in their incomes from 1983 to 1993 and then another 9 percent rise from 1993 to 2005. But even this undercounts the actual gains, because the number of people living in low income households has been shrinking as a result of the breakdown of the family, people having fewer children, and more people living alone.

Is this a 'winner-take-all' society?

Not winner-take-all, but there is no question that in America today those who have superior talents and are the best or near-best at what they do—surgeons, lawyers, athletes, entertainers, and so forth—earn a big premium above those who are only average or even above average in these professions. While the first pick in the NFL draft might sign a $60 million contract, the 40th pick in the draft may not even make the team.

This is a consequence of an information age and a global economy where talent and celebrity pay very large dividends. And, admittedly, it doesn't always seem fair.

Are the income gaps between races and between sexes increasing or decreasing?

Here we have very positive news. Since 1980, women have seen much faster income gains than men, and blacks have made faster gains than whites. White males still earn the most, but the gap is narrowing significantly. What this means is that the "gaps" in pay today are more likely to be a result of one's skills and productivity, not so much the color of one's skin or one's gender.

Since 1980, the median income for black households has risen by 28 percent; Hispanic households by 17 percent; and white households by 16 percent.

Are high tax rates on the rich a good way to redistribute income?

No. History teaches us that high tax rates are the worst way to redistribute income to the poor and the middle class. I recently reviewed IRS tax return data by income group going back to 1972. The results are jaw-dropping. In 1972, when the highest tax rate on the rich was 70 percent and the top capital gains tax rate was 35 percent, the richest 1 percent of Americans paid 17 percent of the income tax burden. Today, with a top income tax rate of 35 percent and capital gains at 15 percent, they pay 39 percent. With higher income tax rates the rich shelter more of their income through tax carve-outs, they invest less in the United States and more abroad, and they work less. The Robin Hood strategy has almost always failed because it means less income, not more, to take from the rich and give to the poor.

For Further Discussion

1. Chapter 1 describes the living and working conditions of California migrant workers during the 1930s. How does this background information help readers better understand the characters of George and Lennie in the novel?

2. Numerous articles in Chapter 2 express the opinion that in *Of Mice and Men* the American dream is presented as an illusion, a goal that remains stubbornly out of reach. Review *Of Mice and Men*, and define the dreams of the various characters. Next, refer to the viewpoints by Kenneth D. Swan, Frederick I. Carpenter, Duncan Reith, and Louis Owens and describe their differing reasons for why they believe these dreams are unattainable for the characters.

3. John H. Timmerman and Peter Lisca's viewpoints in Chapter 2 explore how Steinbeck's creative choices in *Of Mice and Men* lend meaning to the work. They claim that foreshadowing, framing, and the use of recurring motifs create levels of richness in the novel. Using these viewpoints as a guide, think about what other elements of fiction are at work in the book. How, for example, does Steinbeck develop characters that are sympathetic? How does the novel's various crises, climax, and resolution help further the theme of thwarted dreams?

4. Charlotte Cook Hadella's and Lesley Broder's essays in Chapter 2 critically examine the character of Curley's wife in *Of Mice and Men*. Refer to these articles to explain how this character's vision of the American dream differs from or is similar to the dreams of the men in the novel. Why is it significant that she is the only female character in the novel, and why does she remain unnamed?

5. In her article in Chapter 2, Winifred Dusenbury Frazer explains that homelessness creates loneliness for the characters in *Of Mice and Men*. In Chapter 3, David Kamp and Peter C. Whybrow also discuss Americans' emotional need for not just a home, but bigger homes with expensive amenities, at any cost. Examine these articles to discern why homeownership is such an integral part of the American dream. How would owning land and a home change George and Lennie's lives in the novel? What does home ownership represent for Americans today?

6. In his selection in Chapter 3, Stephen Moore explains the climate of the American dream in the United States today. Using Moore's article as a guide, discuss whether Americans' grasp on the American dream today seems any stronger than it was for Steinbeck's migrant characters from the 1930s. Are people today more or less able to fulfill their dreams?

For Further Reading

William Durbin, *The Journal of C.J. Jackson, a Dust Bowl Migrant, Oklahoma to California, 1935*. New York: Scholastic, 2002.

Gerald Haslam, *Snapshots*. Walnut Creek, CA: Devil Mountain Books, 1985.

————, *That Constant Coyote: California Stories*. Las Vegas: University of Nevada Press, 1990.

John Steinbeck, *Cannery Row*. New York: Viking, 1945.

————, *East of Eden*. New York: Viking, 1952.

————, *The Grapes of Wrath*. London: Heinemann, 1939.

————, *In Dubious Battle*. New York: Covici-Friede, 1936.

————, *The Pearl*. New York: Viking, 1948.

————, *Tortilla Flat*. New York: Modern Library, 1935.

Celia Strang, *Foster Mary*. New York: McGraw Hill, 1979.

Ronald B. Taylor, *Long Road Home*. New York: Henry Holt, 1989.

Theodore Taylor, *The Maldonado Miracle*. New York: Houghton Mifflin, 2003.

Bibliography

Books

Jackson J. Benson   *The Short Novels of John Steinbeck: Critical Essays with a Checklist to Steinbeck Criticism.* Durham, NC: Duke University Press, 1990.

Harold Bloom   *John Steinbeck's "Of Mice and Men."* New York: Chelsea House, 2006.

Barbara Ehrenreich   *Bait and Switch: The (Futile) Pursuit of the American Dream.* New York: Henry Holt, 2005.

Ruben Martinez   *Crossing Over: A Mexican Family on the Migrant Trail.* New York: Metropolitan Books, 2001.

Debra McArthur   *John Steinbeck: "The Grapes of Wrath" and "Of Mice and Men."* New York: Marshall Cavendish Benchmark, 2009.

Michael J. Meyer   *The Essential Criticism of John Steinbeck's "Of Mice and Men."* Lanham, MD: Scarecrow, 2009.

Barack Obama   *The Audacity of Hope: Thoughts on Reclaiming the American Dream.* New York: Random House, 2006.

Susan Shillinglaw   *Beyond Boundaries: Rereading John Steinbeck.* Tuscaloosa: University of Alabama Press, 2002.

Roy Simmonds	*A Biographical and Critical Introduction of John Steinbeck.* Lewiston, NY: Edwin Mellen Press, 2000.
Earl Smith	*Race, Sport, and the American Dream.* Durham, NC: Carolina Academic Press, 2007.
Bruce Watson	*Bread and Roses: Mills, Migrants, and the Struggle for the American Dream.* New York: Penguin, 2006.

Periodicals

Carolyn M. Brown	"Pursuing the American Dream," *Black Enterprise*, June 2009.
Bert Cardullo	"On the Road to Tragedy: Mice, Candy, and Land in *Of Mice and Men*," *American Drama*, Winter 2007.
Bert Cardullo	"The Past in the Present, the End in the Beginning: The Mouse as Symbol in *Of Mice and Men*," *Notes on Contemporary Literature*, March 1990.
Daniel B. Cornfield	"Ending Poverty in America: How to Restore the American Dream," *Social Forces*, June 2009.
Morris Dickstein	"Steinbeck and the Great Depression," *South Atlantic Quarterly*, Winter 2004.
William Greider	"The Future of the American Dream," *Nation*, May 2009.

Melissa Burdick Harmon	"John Steinbeck: Unlikely Voice of the American Struggle," *Biography*, February 2002.
Sharon Jayson	"The Recession Generation: Those Just Starting Out Find the Game Changed," *USA Today*, June 24, 2009.
Denise Moore	"The Story Behind George Orwell's *Animal Farm*/The Story Behind Mark Twain's *The Adventures of Huckleberry Finn*/The Story Behind John Steinbeck's *Of Mice and Men*," *School Library Journal*, February 2007.
Madeline Mundt	"We Are Americans: Undocumented Students Pursuing the American Dream," *Library Journal*, October 15, 2009.
Louis Owens	"Deadly Kids, Stinking Dogs, and Heroes: The Best Laid Plans in Steinbeck's *Of Mice and Men*," *Steinbeck Studies*, Fall 2002.
John Petrick	"Matters of Commitment: And of the American Dream in *Of Mice and Men*," *Bergen County (NJ) Record*, September 3, 2004.
Elton Robinson	"Italian Families Parlay Hard Work into a Piece of the American Dream," *Southeast Farm Press*, February 14, 2007.

Hannah Strange   "Migrant Workers Fall Prey to
                      Kidnap Gangs as They Chase
                      American Dream," *Times* (London),
                      October 10, 2009.

Index